Marilyn Lives!

All photographs are from private collectors with the exception of the following:

George Barris: *Front Cover, p. 17*
Henri Dauman/Magnum: *pp. 108–109*
Kobal Collection: *pp. 6–7, pp. 22–23, p. 26, p. 27, p. 29, p. 31, p. 48, p. 57, p. 71, p. 95, p. 114*
Museum of Modern Art Film Stills Archive: *pp. 12–13, p. 16, pp. 34–35, p. 38, p. 41, p. 44, p. 53, p. 55, pp. 72–73, pp. 74–75, pp. 76–77, p. 80, p.94*
Pictorial Parade: *p. 39, p. 46, p. 51, p. 111, pp. 112–113, p. 121*
Harvey Wang: *pp. 14–15*
Wide World: *p. 79*

MARILYN LIVES! (The Photographs)

On Screen:

Bus Stop: pp. 40-41, p. 45; *Gentlemen Prefer Blondes:* p. 36, p. 38; *How to Marry a Millionaire;* with co-stars Lauren Bacall and Betty Grable: p. 81;
Let's Make Love: p. 43; *The Misfits:* pp. 102-107; *The Prince and the Showgirl:* p. 50, p. 72; *River of No Return:* pp. 33-35;
The Seven Year Itch: pp. 66-67, p. 79; *Some Like It Hot:* p. 51, pp. 74-77; *Something's Got To Give*, never released: pp. 118-119.

Off Screen

Norma Jean: pp. 18-19; USO Show in Korea, 1954: pp. 46-47; Marilyn and her men, husbands James Dougherty, Joe DiMaggio and Arthur Miller: pp. 70-71;
Singing Happy Birthday to President Kennedy: p. 100; Marilyn and Arthur Miller: pp. 108-109, p. 111; A fan in her footsteps, Hollywood's famed Chinese Theater: p. 121.

Special thanks to: Wesley Goodwin, Neal Peters, Steve Hoffman

Copyright © Joel Oppenheimer 1981
All rights reserved

ISBN#: 0-933328-02-8

Library of Congress Catalog Card Number: 81-67642

Delilah Books
A Division of Delilah Communications Ltd.
118 E. 25th St., New York, N.Y. 10010

First printing 1981
Manufactured in the United States of America

Front cover design by Steve Hoffman
Back cover and book design by Ed Caraeff

Marilyn Lives!
BY JOEL OPPENHEIMER

Delilah Books
NEW YORK
Distributed by G. P. Putnam's Sons

Front cover photograph by George Barris

The Thirty Year Itch

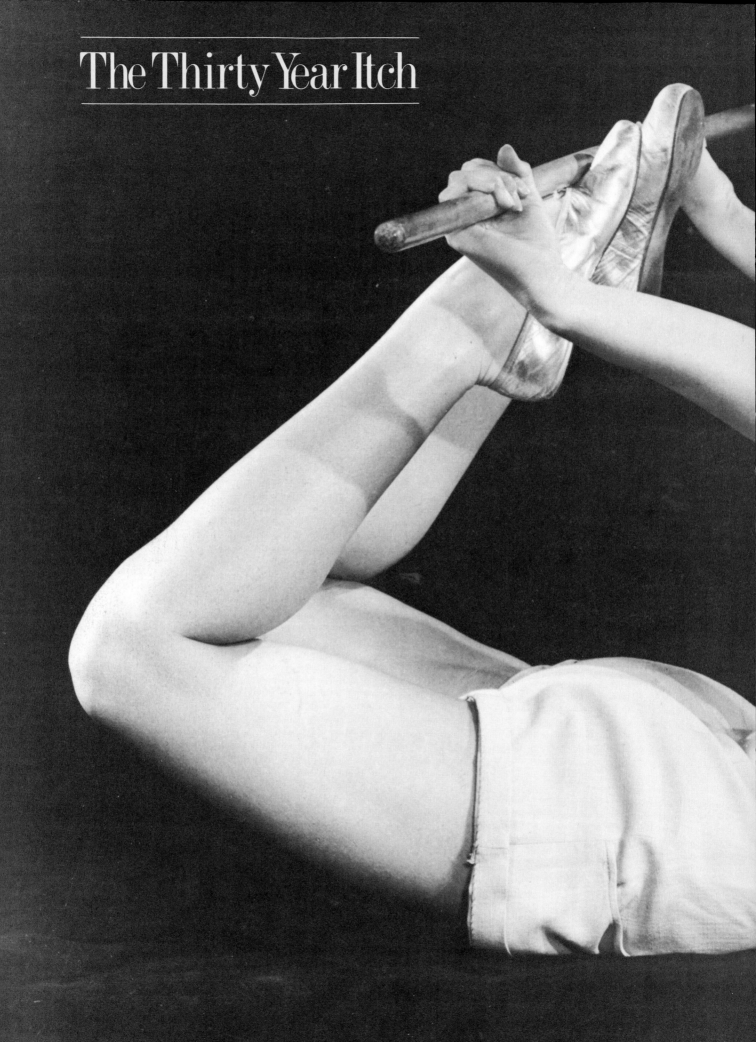

Views From

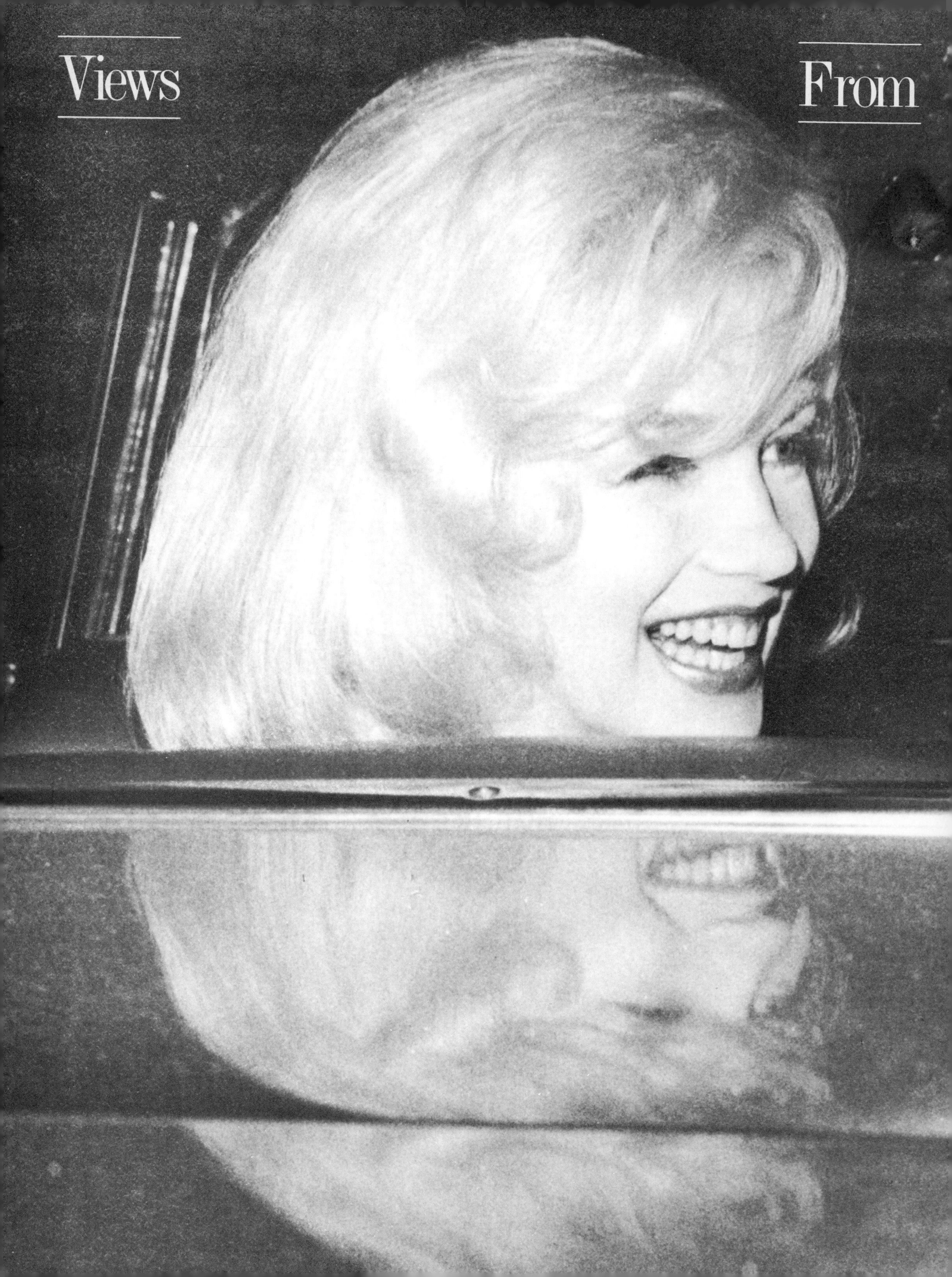

Other Bridges

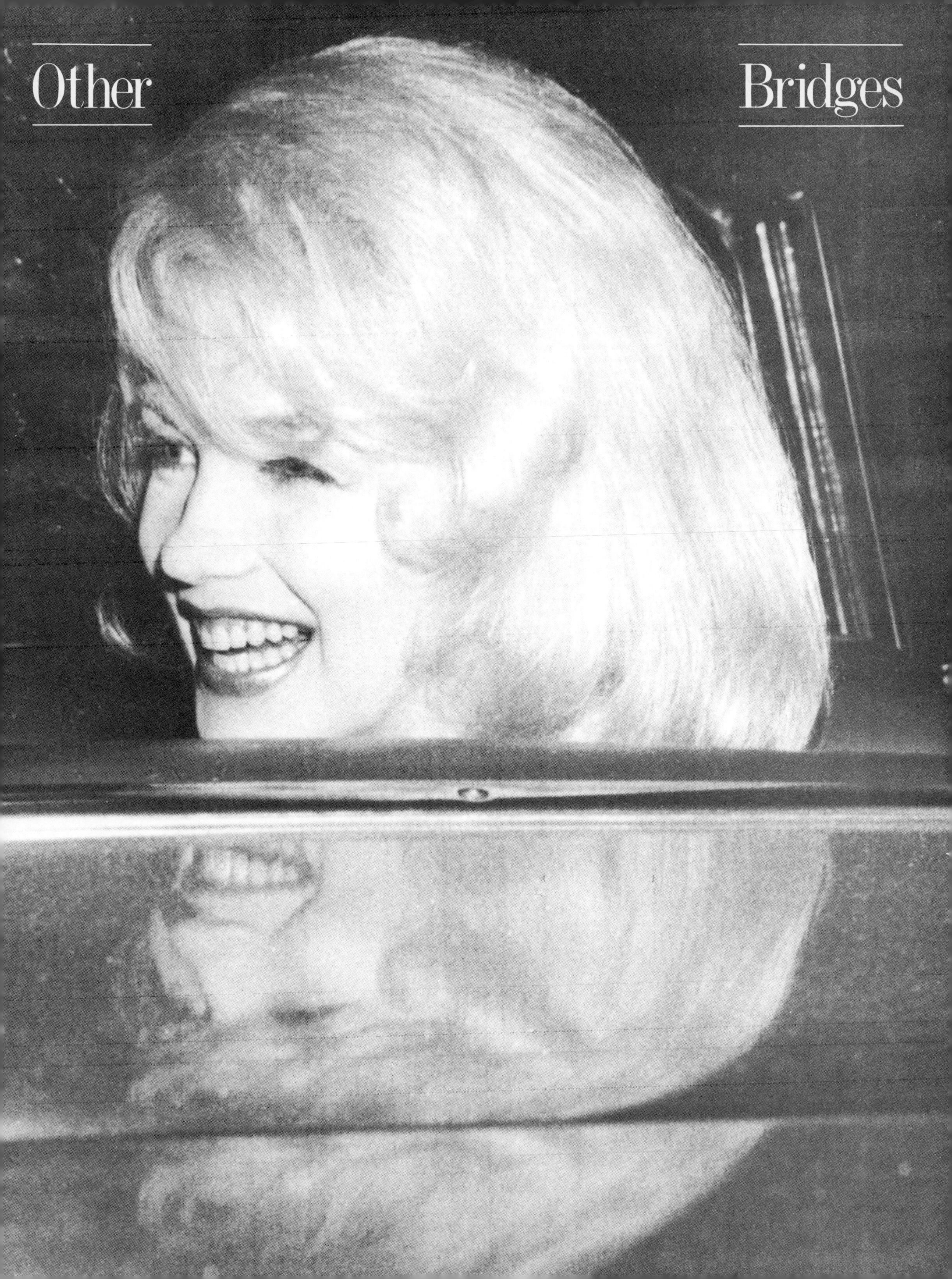

Love And All

*"She looked like, if you bit her,
milk and honey would flow from her"*

The Thirty Year Itch

Why yet another book on Marilyn Monroe? Because she's there, I suppose. Or rather, she's here, in our minds, and in the air around us. She died two decades·ago, in August of 1962, and those two decades have seen enormous changes in our lives; she has remained a constant. In the months that I've been working on this book, I've had a chance to refresh my own memories with re-runs of most of her movies on television; my clip file which I assumed would be meager, is instead bulging. Items about her life and loves as detailed in other people's autobiographies, items about her still unsettled will, all this and more attest to her continuing presence.

I watched her in *"Some Like It Hot"* one night -- and found myself just as turned on during the love scene with Tony Curtis as I had been a quarter of a century ago! That face, those lips, that body (encased in that marvelous gown!), most of all the real woman who presented herself to me and all who watched...and the equally delicious sense of humor that bounced through the whole movie, more than holding its own with Curtis and Lemmon!

Again, on another night, it was *"Bus Stop."* And, again, I was warmed, aroused, taken entirely, by this child-woman-mother. The script creaked a little, you could see the seams where the plot was put together, but Marilyn was as fresh as on first viewing, her singing as beautifully awful, sadly serious, uproariously funny as ever.

I could go on and on about the movies, just as we all can. Everybody who's ever watched her has one scene at least that encapsulates what she was to each of them. Some of the people I talk to in this book mention their favorites. And, as with any great artist, no two agree on which is the best, the

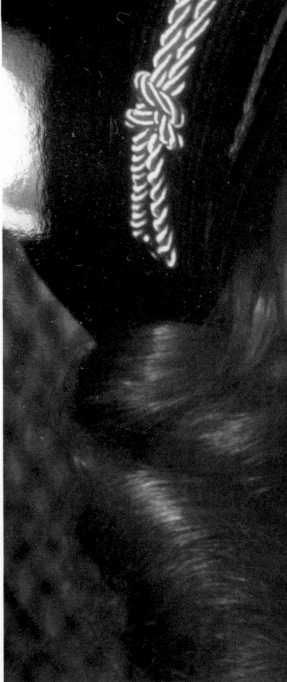

most quintessential. But that's as it should be, because she was so variegated, so diverse and rich in her talents. Just as her life itself was rich, full, intriguing -- and, in the end, sad. Millions of words have been written about that life, the whys and the wherefores, the howcomes and the guesses. The human mind being what it is, there are those who just won't be satisfied until they know for sure who the last phone call went to, who she actually slept with, how she was in bed, and all the rest.

But I didn't want to write a book about Marilyn herself -- first of all I never met her!; secondly, those details, perceptions, and theories don't in-terest me. I suspect that there are many others who feel just as bored with those. The fascination is, certainly, with her -- but more with her fascination for *us* than with the sordid details of how and why she died, how and why she lived. In other words, the story is in how she moved us, and not simply in how she moved.

So I started talking to people. People who still lov-ed her, cared about her, and who had been moved by her during the course of their own lives. Ob-viously I was one of those people.

I suppose I had been aware of Marilyn since the

beginning, the beginning of her career, that is. I'd heard the good words for her brief early appearances in films like *"Love Happy"* -- that wonderful short scene with Groucho -- and I must have seen pictures of her in the magazines and newspapers of the late forties and early fifties. But those years were the beginning of my adult life --I'd turned eighteen in '48 -- and between college and work and marrying and starting a family, the deeply ingrained movie-going habit of my teens had of necessity been broken.

In the autumn of '54 I was working as the advertising production manager of a large but rapidly shrinking schlock furniture chain in Manhattan. Such a job might have been relatively exotic except for two things. It paid all of $60 a week, and the office was located in the heart of the garment district. I was only a fifteen minute walk from Madison Avenue's high glamour, but it might as well have been a cross-country trek.

Every morning I wended my weary way through the racks and hand trucks and dollies hung with, crammed with, piled high with next season's fashions and this season's fabrics. I'd walk past the same small group of men who seemed to have nothing, ever, to do but haggle over the strings of fur tails draped over their shoulders; I'd pass the cafeterias with their double taps, one for water, one for seltzer. The delivery trucks, big and little, blocked the crosswalks, the sidewalks, the intersections. We used to say that if the Russians did invade -- those were the days of the Cold War, remember -- they'd never make it through the traffic on 38th Street.

Once in a while I'd catch a glimpse, as a truck door swung open, of some pin-up or another. It would register for a second and then I'd walk by. I have never been averse to looking at pictures of pretty ladies, and particularly pretty ladies naked. There's no deep psychological or psychoanalytic explanation needed, either: as the youngest of an all-boy family I'd never had an older sister to spy on, and as a depression baby I had none of the advantages of today's *Playboy* and *Penthouse*. One might guess that I'd be eternally curious as to what "they" looked like.

And so, one warm day, as I walked by on my way to work, head filled with the poem I'd been struggling with the night before in my Lower East Side tenement apartment, a guy opened his truck door to start unloading, and my eyes opened to a whole new world. It was a world of mystery and beauty and even, I've come to think, love. It was Marilyn, of course, ripped timely from *Playboy*'s reprint of

her famous calendar. I didn't know that then; what I saw was a lady displayed gloriously, a lady who was gloriously naked, gloriously beautiful, and with a face that was totally unlike any I'd seen in photographs of naked ladies up till then.

Those were lean days for young men who liked to look at unclothed ladies. Not only had we been lacking *Playboy* and *Penthouse*, but most of us had been reared on Sears Catalogs, with their pages of underwear ads, or, around New York City, on the sophisticated bra and girdle ads in The *New York Sunday Times*. Lenny Bruce used to talk about a generation of males being raised to believe that women had staples in their belly buttons; we all thought women came permanently encased in rubber, silk, and snaps. Of course, once in a while we'd fall upon a tattered girlie magazine -- *The Police Gazette*, perhaps -- and get a little closer to the real truth. But magazines like that were hard to come by for teenagers, and, further, most of those women had strange hard faces and looks that were patently put on. There were stock poses. Outraged Innocence, Coy Come-Hither, Brazen Arrogance. The costumes were theatrical, glittery, sexually provocative but not terribly revealing. We learned to settle for the curve of a buttock or a glimpse of breast, or angle or cut of clothes, because if we had been allowed to see a nipple we might have turned into raging maniacs.

So nakedness was non-existent for us young men in those days. Like the radio dramas we'd grown up on, much had to be imagined on the basis of the little revealed. I won't debate the virtues of this approach -- and certainly virtues there are. These days, surrounded by acres and acres of bare flesh in magazines and movies, even ads, one wearies sometimes of it, and wishes for a little forbearance, a touch of the old magic of hidden mysteries. But then we were desperate for the real thing. "Just let me see it!" little boys would pray, not even sure what *it* was. I've met men just slightly older than myself who've never seen their own wives in the altogether, because they had both been taught that nakedness would destroy the romance!

So, that morning, sleep in my eyes and poetry in my head, to see this pure lady in her nakedness was more than shock. It was revelation. And that revelation has held up, has grown in fact, through almost thirty years. Always, since that day, she's been the Goddess, the naked, vulnerable, complete, innocent, and offering Goddess we didn't even know we lusted after or adored.

And *that's* what I'd like this book to be about. That's why it isn't about Marilyn herself; she's been talked about in that way too much already, the many "Marilyn I knew" and the "what she was like" books. And it isn't about the people I'll quote in this book, or about me either. We all just happened to be around at the right time to become lovers, worshippers, awestruck acolytes.

Make no mistake about it: people were awe-struck. Franz Kline was a painter, I think a great one. As a leading member of the New York School, the Abstract-Expressionists, he moved in high circles, ran with the famous and the rich and the powerful. They wanted to know the famous artist, and Franz put up with it, because the prices they paid for his paintings allowed him to paint more of them. And to me, the young poet who was in awe of him, it seemed the proper prerequisite for one who'd worked hard at his art all his life.

Franz got a place out in the Hamptons, finally; all the successful painters did that then, just as now.

"I've always linked her with Jacqueline Kennedy in my mind, because I see them as the two poles of a single experience: the woman who really plays ball with her culture. At one end we have the winner, Jackie Onassis—and at the other end Marilyn, who I imagine kept trying actually to be loved for herself!"

But now anybody who has any money at all goes out there; in the fifties only the very rich and the artists did. The rich lived in huge seaside villas; the painters found old houses, little shacks, out-buildings on the potato farms, and found a way to beat the heat and keep on painting.

Then the word spread among the moneyed ones that there was culture out there in the boondocks, and the rich ladies would spend some of their sum-mer visiting studies and collecting paintings, and sometimes painters, for a summer's dalliance. Franz got his share of these visits and was as bored by them, finally, as any reasonable man who just wanted to do his work would be. So when the phone rang one morning, disturbing his work ses-sion, he answered it wearily. It was a Mrs. Miller, so-and-so had recommended that she see his pain-tings, could she come by, etc., etc., etc. It was a problem, said Franz, later, because it took up your time, and the conversation was usually abomina-ble, and their manners were invariably awful, but they did spend money.

So he said yes. And, of course, when the lady ar-rived the next day as scheduled, it was Marilyn. Franz and I were talking a week or so later in a bar in the city -- poets didn't get out of the summer heat that easily -- when he told me this. He said, "It was Marilyn Monroe, damn it! How was I to know who Mrs. Miller was?" I asked, "But what did she look like? What did she really look like?"

He said, "She looked like, if you bit her, milk and honey would flow from her..." And we both stared into our drinks and then had another. And sat there in silence, thinking about Marilyn.

As far as I'm concerned that kind of thing is the "truth" about Marilyn. It's always the myth that contains the real truth, as opposed to so-called "fact." Myth is our way of interpreting the world, of explaining the unexplainable. We sophisticates keep laughing at myth, at its seeming naivete, and yet time and time again we discover that we're the naifs, and the myth is sophisticated.

Perhaps Marilyn was, as some have called her, a simple "Hollywood Hooker;" perhaps she was selfish, vain, any of the awful things we've been told about her. Certainly she was a little lost in this world, or she wouldn't have committed suicide. But more surely than any of these things she was, and is, what we conceive her to be. She is the myth, because that is what we see, and respond to.

What I've discovered, and I hope you'll see too, in the course of this book, is a Marilyn who besides being that particular kind of myth, a superstar, is a myth in every sense of the word. She is, I think, a personification of the Great Mother, the Mother Goddess who's been worshipped since the dawn of time.

I think you'll hear the people in this book talk about her that way, too. They may not always realize it, but when they speak of the effect she had on them, the various meanings she had in their lives, we begin to realize that she's more than just a media hype or another very pretty face.

Certainly Marilyn had a legendary list of lovers -- a prerequisite for any mother goddess. We know the rumors about Jack Kennedy, the torrid fling with Yves Montand, the snickering about Gable's fatal heart attack, all that. Now Shelley Winters has entered the fray with a list that she says Marilyn drew up one day while the two of them were discussing man troubles.

She says Marilyn asked, "Wouldn't it be nice to be like men, just getting notches in your belt, having affairs with the most attractive men -- and not get-ting emotionally involved?" Ms. Winters says they both loved the idea, and so they each drew up a list of men they'd like to have.

Marilyn's included Zero Mostel, Eli Wallach, Charles Boyer, Jean Renoir, Lee Strassberg, Elia Kazan, Harry Belafonte, Yves Montand, Charles Bickford, Ernest Hemingway, Charles Laughton, Arthur Miller and Albert Einstein. Now, in the first place, that's quite a list for a simple Hollywood Hooker! There is, you'll notice, a wide range of ages, talents, and even physical looks. There is, of course, a heavy preponderance of show business people, but even those are not the usual run of handsome hunks.

But to find Einstein at the end of the list is real stunner. Winters says she said, "Marilyn! There's no way you can have a love affair with Einstein! He's the most famous scientist of our century, and besides, he's an old man!" Marilyn is supposed to have answered, "That has nothing to do with it. I hear he's very young for his age."

And of course she was right. Age did have nothing to do with it, nor, I might add, did the fact of his fame or his field of work. After all, one has to assume that scientists are mortal too, and just as much prey to the ravages of love and desire as other, lesser mortals -- not to mention that fame would be far less of an ego-trip for an Einstein than for a performing artist. And we do know that the old man was deeply concerned with his, and our, mortality. There's a beautiful story about him showing up one morning looking terribly worn and

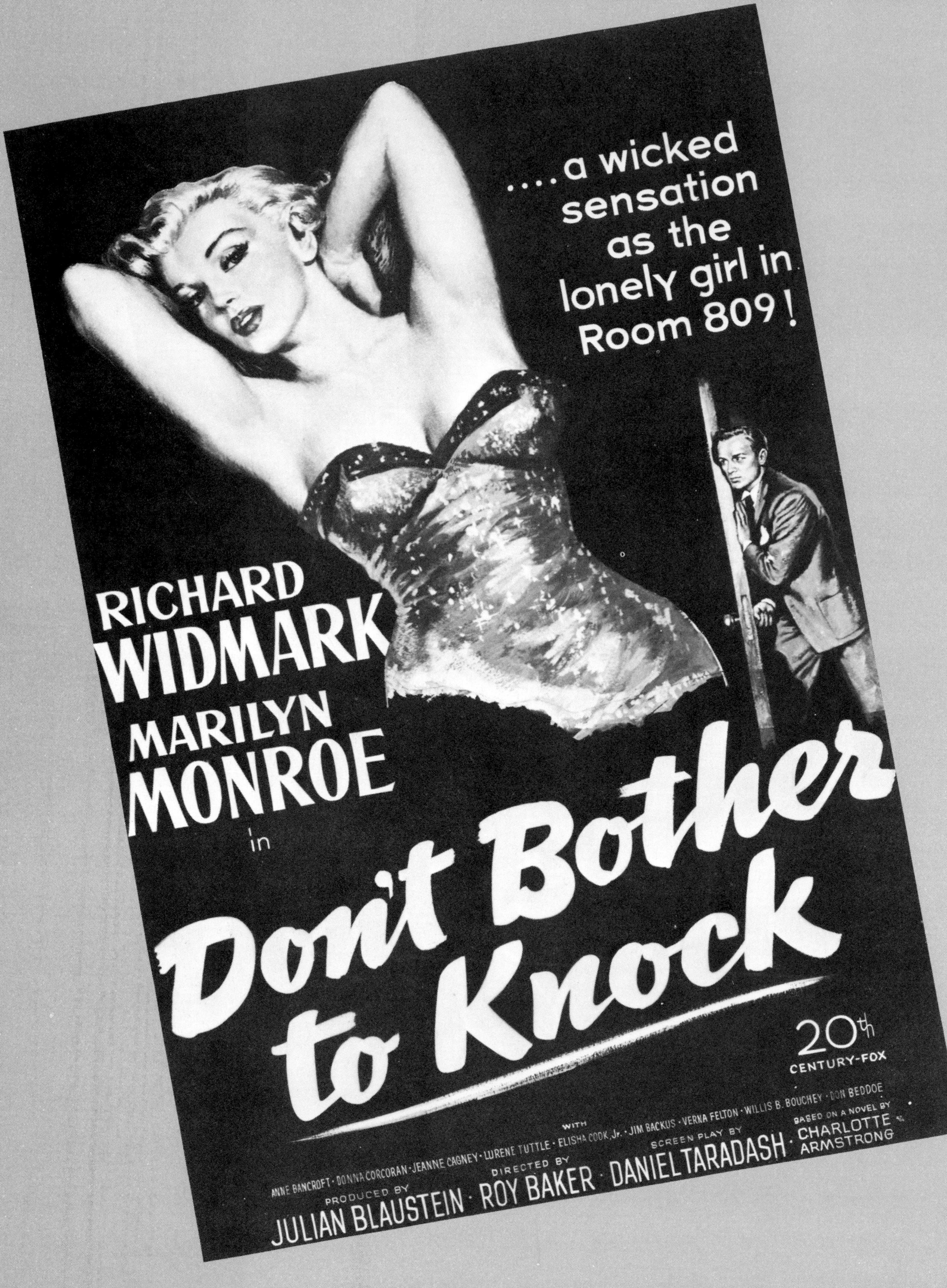

....a wicked sensation as the lonely girl in Room 809!
RICHARD WIDMARK
MARILYN MONROE
in
Don't Bother to Knock
20th CENTURY-FOX
WITH
ANNE BANCROFT · DONNA CORCORAN · JEANNE CAGNEY · LURENE TUTTLE · ELISHA COOK, Jr. · JIM BACKUS · VERNA FELTON · WILLIS B. BOUCHEY · DON BEDDOE
PRODUCED BY JULIAN BLAUSTEIN · DIRECTED BY ROY BAKER · SCREEN PLAY BY DANIEL TARADASH · BASED ON A NOVEL BY CHARLOTTE ARMSTRONG

haggard. An assistant asked him if he were ill; he said, "No, I just didn't sleep much last night. I got into bed, and I started thinking about the universe and suddenly I got terrified that I would fall through..."

I see no reason why he shouldn't be on the list. In fact I'm delighted that he is. And now he will be part of her myth. Although Winters never says Marilyn made it with any of these people, or even that she tried -- she just says that they were on the list of men she wanted -- within weeks of the appearance of the story I heard people casually taking it for granted that Marilyn had indeed been to bed with Einstein.

Once again, myth versus reality. Yet people seem to want to believe that Marilyn made love with everybody. It goes with the territory if you're Aphrodite or Astarte. People seem to feel that Marilyn was entitled to her lovers -- as opposed to the way they will talk about an Elizabeth Taylor, for example. All the other stars we're aware of are seen either as "pure" or as "sluts." Marilyn is seen as both good and sexual at the same time, and she is excused what in others is mortal sin, or at least bad taste. Marilyn is moral and amoral, clean and dirty, woman complete and incarnate in all woman's forms. And that, my friends, is the definition of the Mother Goddess. She just isn't always nice, she isn't always loving and giving. Sometimes she hurts us, or ignores us, or even double-crosses us. And we expect that kind of behavior, even if we don't always want it to be so.

And there *was* a large framed portrait of Einstein among Marilyn's possessions at the time of her death. It's supposed to have been signed "To Marilyn, with respect and love and thanks." It's always possible that all she did was write him a fan letter, because there are lots of people who have signed pictures from her with personal messages who never saw her either. But if that's the case, that's good enough for me. In fact it's kind of terrific, that she would write the old man. And if she did rouse him to heights of passion, that's even better.

Well, that's all part of the myth, or fact, whichever. In an attempt to begin to see her as we saw her then, I visited Jack Banning, who runs a store called *Yesterday* specializing in posters from the not too distant past, or, in other words, nostalgia. I've known Jack since the days when he was in public relations and I knew in a vague way that Marilyn had been partly responsible for his shift from that world into this new one of 'chic' small businessman; I thought I'd like to hear about how that happened, and see if he had garnered any

insights into the myth from the business. He said, "The way I got into collecting Marilyn stuff was very simple. The first Christmas that my wife Sandra and I were together, about twelve years ago, I decided I wanted a James Dean poster and a Marilyn one too. Now that we're in the business we know that that's a fairly typical kind of collection. People who are into the fifties tend to be more interested in those two than Brando or Judy Garland or some of the others. There's a fifties mentality that calls for those two.

"So Sandra found me a *Rebel Without a Cause* poster, and a *Don't Bother To Knock* one. We had them plastic-covered and stuck them on the walls of the bedroom, and they're still up there, even though we've been through thousands of posters and thousands of incarnations ourselves. That's how we got started.

"After that I just decided it would be fun -- in a stamp collector sort of way -- to accumulate every poster on which Marilyn appeared, as much for the challenge as anything else."

It occurred to me that it was indeed Marilyn he wanted to collect, rather than anybody else, so it wasn't just "stamp collecting!" But I didn't go in-

to that aspect of it yet. I asked instead if it had got boring, just collecting one face over and over. His answer was particularly revealing. "On some pictures we have a number of posters -- I think on *River Of No Return* for example, we have a French poster, an Italian poster, a German one and several American ones. All of them handle the exploitation a different way. You can see the emotional differences: the French posters are always line-drawn and show the body in a very curvaceous way; the Italians do much more with the face and hair -- they make a mane of hair on her. The Americans were much more photographic in their presentation.

"You could say I began to get interested in the popular culture aspects of the poster business, particularly in the exploitation angle from the advertising and promotion end. That's what I used to be in myself. The question of how did they exploit this character -- Marilyn. That's why I never got deep into still photos or the celluloid itself. I was always interested in the advertisement; it was all about how you got people to respond in a very direct way. And the other thing was covers of magazines, not the inside stories. The inside stories were one thing, but the cover was how they were getting you to buy this magazine! And that always fascinated me."

But this interest had come later in his life for him, after he was already embarked on a career. I asked him if he had had an earlier interest in Marilyn, and to talk about that. He said, "When I was in prep school in 1956 or so, I used to write away to Marilyn for signed photographs. They always came through with the secretarial signatures in red ballpen! You can always recognize that...you'd get one that said 'Best Wishes, Marilyn Monroe,' the first one. Then you'd write again and ask for another picture and say 'Couldn't you write something a little more personal?' and it would come back signed 'To Jack -- best wishes, Marilyn Monroe,' and you'd say to yourself well that's still a little formal, so you'd write away again, still asking for something more personal. After about six months of this I finally got up to 'Love and kisses, Marilyn' -- which for a kid of fifteen was the ultimate! But I never thought about her after that -- at least in terms of collecting -- until I decided I wanted the poster.

"I was never a movie-goer at that age and I was more fascinated with the calendar, the nude. At that time, in the early fifties she was in all those tiny 10-cent magazines, *Tempo, Quick*, I forget all the names. But she was always on the cover, and in features in them. That was the attraction for me, Marilyn as pin-up. I never thought of her as being a movie star! I didn't see her that way. The calendar

had been shot in '49, of course, and they released it in '52, and then it was really big in '54 after *Playboy* reprinted it. Every barber shop, every tire store, everybody had it up on the wall. But I knew her before that! All the bathing suit shots in those magazines. I remember there was a whole lot in plastic see-through shoes. My first recollection of her as a pin-up name is in '51 or '52, I think.

"She'd already started in the movies of course, and had gotten a lot of play about that, with *Asphalt Jungle* and *Love Happy*, and then they re-released them when she became bigger. Even *Ladies Of The Chorus,* which she made in '48, I think, where she got second billing, they reissued in '51 or '52. The first big picture where anybody took her seriously as an actress wasn't really, I guess, until *Some Like It Hot.* Anyhow, between prep school, which was strict about such things, and earlier Friday and Saturday nights being make-out nights, I just didn't get to the movies very much. So I only knew people like Marilyn and Brigitte Bardot through pin-ups.

"And of course as far as my ultimate motive went then, magazines were better than movie memories...Marilyn, Brigitte, Ursula Andress -- I was never put off by any of them.

"Now when I got back into this stuff I don't think I was turned on again as I had been. I think it was purely intellectual this time around. But, on the other hand, about three years ago I stumbled on a whole cache of Brigitte's posters from those days, and they are still sensationally sexy! They're posters you'd respond to today -- and that you'd respond to if you were ninety-five years old!

"Brigitte was really the pure sex-goddess and Marilyn was that and more. Maybe in the early to mid-fifties you could think that she was just sex. But then, after DiMaggio, and after *The Prince*

And The Showgirl, and then into *The Misfits,* while the myth was taking hold, all the heavy stuff started to come down, and it became something else. I didn't respond to her any more on the personal level. And I have a sneaking suspicion that the presentation of her changed too then, in the posters. I have a feeling she was handled differently.

"The early stuff was sex goddess, sort of cute sex goddess, girl next door stuff. Later on it was much more exalted. Although I have to say that the skirt-blowing scene, the poster for *Seven Year Itch,* at first I thought it was just straight peek-a-boo stuff, and now we look at it as a serious cultural phenomenon!"

"Well," I interjected, "it was! But of course it wasn't perceived as such." And that weighty statement stopped Jack for a second. To get him started again I mentioned one of my favorite posters, that of Rita Hayworth as "Gilda," and how that poster was clearly Hayworth playing a part, acting.

"Sure. But Marilyn was always Marilyn, there was always substance to her, and whatever it was, it's what keeps her alive today."

What kind of people does Jack see in his store, looking for Marilyn? He says most of them are middle-aged, male, gay, but he's quick to point out that the store's location and "seriousness" and the fair amount of sophistication, and the prices, too, may be keeping young people away. But in keeping an eye on friendly competitors, he says he notices that the poster shops which aim at kids always have some Marilyns up there among Charlie's Angels and Raquel, Farrah, and the rest. He ended by noting that everybody seemed to respond to her, men and women, young and old. Of course, that's how The Great Mother works!

Young Love

ow I wanted to talk to the fans, the ones who loved Marilyn then, and still loved her now, twenty years later. I found some who hadn't felt themselves affected by her while she was alive, but now gobbled up her pictures, but there were almost none who were the reverse, who'd cared then, and forgotten her now. Like all good legends, she seems to be growing rather than diminishing.

Claire is a woman in her thirties who works in what we call "communications." She's attractive and bright and she agreed to sit down and try to figure out her feelings, recall her memories about Marilyn.

"I was probably eight years old...my father took me to Madison Square Garden and just before the entrance, at the old Garden at 50th Street, there was a soda fountain, and I remember passing this window of the fountain and seeing this calendar in it. My father pulled me away, but I wanted to stop and look at it! I remember seeing her! It must have been something special to me...I remember the red background. I don't remember much else from that incident, like why it moved me or anything, but it must have had a big influence on me to keep remembering it.

"A couple of years later I went to see *Gentlemen Prefer Blondes*. I was really enchanted with her. I was around twelve, a real tomboy, but just beginning to be aware of sexuality. Elvis Presley was around too, and between him and her, well, they were the ones who gave me those strange feelings. The thing I remember most was when I was twelve and a half, I went to a party, and I did an imitation of Marilyn. I swept my hair back -- the transition from tomboy had been very quick! -- and stood in front of everybody with my hands on my knees and my ass sticking out, I didn't have much of a chest

at the time, of course, and I started to sing a song --I can't remember, but I think it was *I Want To Be Loved By You,* but she might have done that later -- anyhow I sang it with a real breathy kind of voice and that sort of poutiness Marilyn had. The whole thing was to be enticing to men. And I was twelve and a half.

"I thought it was great -- and it worked! I didn't know what to do in order to be popular until I found out about Marilyn Monroe. I loved the way she looked and I knew she had something.

"So she was a sexual role model for me -- not how to be a grown-up woman, but how to be a sexual woman. There was something in her that made me feel she had real power, she got what she wanted without having to do anything else, just look a certain way and be a certain way.

"There were other movie stars, too, who affected me, but in different ways. Katherine Hepburn, Bette Davis —and Loretta Young because she looked like my mother—but they were different, they weren't sexual.

"It seemed as if Marilyn could get whatever she wanted, and I took something from that, because it was an easy way to get favors, to get things, and you didn't have to work real hard at it. And at that time, I didn't believe in anything else about myself. It took a long time for that to change, but then, being sexual was a real good way to get attention fast!

"So she really had an impact on me. I looked for her movies, I checked all the magazines, but I didn't write her, I thought that was nonsense, that was for fanatics."

I asked Claire if she'd been bugged by Marilyn's lushness, since she was then a skinny tomboy -- and is still, now quite slender. "No," she said, "I wanted to be like her. I couldn't wait."

We talked then for a little about how many of us felt un-beautiful when young, and how we had nobody to talk to about it. Claire says she had one friend who was a little older, blonde, and very good-looking and she suspects now that they were friends just because the girl was like that. But, in any event, Marilyn became the desired ideal. Claire wanted to be beautiful.

"I don't think it was the healthiest of models to have, because the only thing I saw was a quick solution to getting something. In a sense it turned out to be quite negative later on. That was the only thing I put emphasis on and it got attention and it got what I wanted very quickly, but behind that there was nothing, before I developed as a person.

"One of the loveliest things about her was that she was accessible to women. The culture kept telling us she was the ultimate sex symbol, the blond bombshell...I never felt excluded by her, not when I was little and she was my Magic Mommy, not when I was older and she was some sort of a sister."

"But of course, later, as I began to grow myself, I saw her differently. In the movies I saw then, I still liked her sexuality, but it was different, because it had a certain kind of innocence to it and you couldn't put any kind of blame on it.

"I remember that my mother liked her, she didn't seem to threaten women. I don't remember my father ever talking about her. But I did have a dream about Marilyn and my father —not what you think! —about three or four weeks ago, before you even mentioned that you wanted to talk to me. I opened a bureau drawer in the attic of our old house in New Jersey and there were pictures of Marilyn Monroe, and I was looking at them. I said 'Hey! Daddy took these pictures!' I said, 'Wow! I can't believe it, Daddy took these pictures of Marilyn Monroe! He knows her! That's terrific!' I was really excited about it.

"And I had another dream about six, seven years ago, about her. In the dream I became Marilyn, but I was still me, too. Somebody murdered me, her I mean, in the dream. Then I read all that stuff about her maybe being murdered, but I didn't think that was what it was about. It just showed how closely I was connected with her."

Everybody I talked to had a favorite movie, of

course, and a favorite scene. With Claire it was *Some Like It Hot,* and the scene was the one with Marilyn and Tony Curtis in the john of the Pullman Car, getting the ice cubes. I mentioned watching the film recently, and how ga-ga I'd been over her love scene with Curtis on the yacht, when she's trying to prove to him that he can be moved physically. She said, "I never watched that scene with as much sexuality as this time. She was really in that scene! She was real happy about doing it, wasn't she?" And I said, "Either that, or the world's greatest actress."

I asked Claire how she felt about Marilyn as an actress, the old argument about whether she took a wrong turn by moving into heavier roles, by trying to be a serious actress. "I liked her in *The Misfits.* I thought that was her best role. The final ten minutes of the movie, when she's trying to stop the killing of the horses, I thought that was one of the best things she'd ever done. All her beauty was there, and her vulnerability, but they come through in a different way than her sexuality. That's what great acting is, letting the emotions out without hiding. And she didn't."

I brought up the Einstein story. Claire said, "It surprised me. But I loved it. I liked Einstein. I'd never make moral judgments about Marilyn anyway. I think she was what every woman wanted to be, in a certain way. That beautiful, and that sexual, and that free with it. She seemed to be able to do such things without judgment from others, although she may have been judging herself. The thing I remember in that light is how sad she was when she split up with Joe DiMaggio, and her hospitalizations. But she never hurt anyone else, she never did anything with the intent to hurt someone else. And if someone had told me that she had I wouldn't have believed it. I guess it's believable. She didn't seem bigger than life, she seemed reachable."

Claire was seventeen when Marilyn died and still very much involved in a sexual image, and she says she felt very very sad. "It seemed like it just shouldn't have happened, like it was all wrong. It didn't make sense that someone like her would be left all alone like that."

That led to Claire talking about how she also related to Marilyn's aloneness. She, like many teenagers, felt lonely and isolated, and that became a connection too. So the slow change in her feelings about Marilyn was beginning. It was no longer just her sexuality, it was her innocence, her vulnerability. The thing she remembers most from the later pictures, was the look of discovery that was always on Marilyn's face when something happened. "It's as though it's the first time it's happened and she's still only four years old. And coupled with her sexuality, that's such a knockout. It's everything!

"And I don't find that innocence, that vulnerability pathetic. It's like she used it, had it, in certain situations -- like *Bus Stop,* but that was part of the role. She never was allowed to be that smart in a movie. Victimized, yes, but not pathetic. She was trapped by a lot of circumstances. She couldn't be alone, and yet she was always alone. I felt for her because I knew she was troubled, and I was very unhappy then too, so I guess it was all tied up together.

"But I also knew I wasn't going to let myself be destroyed. I felt sorry for her that she didn't know how to pull herself out of these overwhelming circumstances, and I guess I thought that I was able to. I'd heard that she spent the last few years of her life very close to a psychiatrist, in his care. I knew I never wanted to get in that position. I just sort of ached for her. I mean she had everything -- everything I wanted -- and I thought those were pretty good things that she had, but she didn't know how to protect herself. And it took me a lot of years to learn that protection was necessary. That you can protect yourself without losing your vulnerability, your innocence. She didn't know how to do that. I think that most people feel that if they put up some sort of protection they'll lose the realness of themselves. But that doesn't make any sense. I still worry about that now. That you can care and feel and show those feelings and yet still maintain yourself. But you have to be smart enough to know what's going on. She never had that opportunity because she was too close to herself. I wouldn't have wanted, now when I think about it, to have had her fame, not the way she had it.

"The thing I remember about photographs of her, some of the late ones, is she still had the sweetness of a child. A sweetness that most sexuality doesn't have. I remember somebody saying Marilyn made everybody want her, but in a way I think women wanted her too. And it was more than sexuality.

"I wish I could have done something to stop it from happening, her dying. I know what men mean when they say they could have saved her. I suspect I'm drawn to her also because I know how men feel about her. That much softness and innocence and sexuality and beauty all together. So much! I remember watching her in *Some Like It Hot* -- she was big! She was not skinny by any means, she was almost fat. She was a Rubens. And totally wonderful. She made that look good. And on somebody else it just would not have worked.

But Marilyn could use all that stuff.

"God, I feel like crying right now, thinking about all this stuff. If you don't talk to anybody about it, you don't know it's there.

"It's as if someone stopped her on purpose, didn't want the dream to go on any further. I've tried to fantasize what she would have been like now, turning into an older woman, and I just can't. Everybody wanted her to be the way she was, and not change. I think she was afraid of changing, and she didn't know how well she was doing it. She didn't know what was underneath all that external stuff.

"It's like when I think of the calendar picture, the thing that started it for me. It's like her body is over here and her face over there looking over her shoulder but disconnected.

"I guess I wanted the kind of love the public gave her. In my younger years I thought that would be terrific. But it isn't."

Claire was nearly in tears when we stopped talking. We were at my place, and my young sons were there, so we managed to pull her out of the depression with a science fiction game and an ABC-TV re-run of Rock and Roll. But Marilyn obviously had been, and was still, more than just another movie star in her life. She'd, literally, helped form her, and taught her, sometimes by hard lessons, how to live her own life.

The next person I talked to had a much different take. Vic is maybe ten years older than Claire, he's a writer and a movie buff, and, clearly, he's a male. He grew up in The Bronx, and he saw

Marilyn for the first time in *Love Happy* -- which of course he'd gone to for Groucho. "I was probably fourteen at the time. She just looked like another great built chick. I remember *Niagara* and her walk -- I was an usher then and we had all that advertising pushing it -- and so we all waited for the walk and there it was, and it was dynamite. Who cared about Joseph Cotten? And that's when I really remember her.

"I never got to her through magazines or pin-ups or anything. I didn't buy movie magazines and *Playboy* wasn't around yet -- or if it was I certainly couldn't've bought it, not in high school. It would have been out of the question in The Bronx! So my take was just through the movies. I'm sure that by *Seven Year Itch* she was the biggest for me, that was the one where she was sensational for me. It wasn't my type, I mean she was awesome and all that and I got to appreciate her more later on. But then I was a hopeless Glynis Johns guy -- I mean I went for the demure types who looked like they had a spark that I could bring out.

"You look back to *Love Happy* and she just looked like a forties broad in it. She didn't look like much, in fact, maybe even a little chubby as I think of her. Maybe not chubby, but not sleek, not overpowering. But then there's some sort of over-night transformation. I didn't see a lot of the films in between, they just weren't that big, but when she finally came around in *Niagara*, *Seven Year Itch*, even *River Of No Return*, she just had become Marilyn Monroe. I mean it just had happened!

"By the time the news filtered down to The Bronx I guess we were maybe the last to know. But the flacks delivered the desired result, they gave you what they promised you. That isn't usually the case -- I mean, Suzanne Sommers, forget it!"

We talked about some of the other sexpots around at the time. Since Vic had worked as an usher he saw a lot of all of them. "I had a terrific feeling for Brigitte. Mansfield was always closer to parody, she was like Mae West. I didn't really have that sexuality thing for actresses, though. I thought they were the size of the Silver Screen, and how could you go to bed with a woman who was thirty-five feet tall? I had enough trouble fantasizing anyway since I didn't have my own room, but Marilyn wasn't one of the fantasy women. Mostly I picked on the local talent, the girls around.

"But I remember her death. Absolutely. A friend and I were at Army Reserve summer camp and there was a work detail we were ducking. We were sitting in the back of a truck that had a flap over it, just having a nice old time. Then a guy stuck his

head in the flap and we got very nervous because we didn't think anybody knew we were there. We said, 'Okay, we're coming right out...', and he said, 'Relax, relax. I just wanted to tell you we just heard Marilyn Monroe died.' It turned out everybody knew we were there. We didn't see a paper the two weeks we were there, but I remember the press coverage was intense, and when I got out I saw a story in *Newsweek* or *Time* about her death. It quoted a *Journal-American* editor as saying, 'I'm sorry she had to die, but if she did, I'm glad it was August!'

"Well, now I've much more understanding of what she was about. As a kid I was just so backward, she was just awesome. But now I can say I don't think anybody has come close to touching her status as the reigning sex queen in the last twenty years. I think *The Misfits* and *Some Like It Hot* are going to be the films that people stay with. She still works for me in them, absolutely. I'm never disappointed. *Misfits* is an impressive film and *Some Like It Hot* is a masterpiece, and she's awfully awfully good in it, she's terrific in it. I also liked her in a very silly movie with Yves Montand, *Let's Make Love*, very silly, very minor. *The Prince and The Showgirl* was a little long for me, a little static. She was really good in *Bus Stop* too. And *Seven Year Itch* is carried by her -- it's such a slender vehicle otherwise, outside of the great title.

"I was thinking about what I'd like to see her in if she was alive today. I saw *Dressed To Kill* and a lot of it is watching Angie Dickinson naked, and they'd be about the same age. Well, if Marilyn'd been alive, Angie Dickinson would've been out of work!"

I mentioned a story to Vic that I'd heard from another friend about being shown around Hollywood by a long-time flack. They were all asking him about the stars, what's so and so like, and all that. It was several years after Marilyn had died but they asked him about her. He said, "Typical uncomplicated Hollywood Hooker 'til the Miller-Strasberg crowd got hold of her." Some people think that has the ring of truth, and sometimes I suspect that Vic's one of them. But faced with his last statement I asked him about that now. He said, "Well, there was that wonderful flap when she said she wanted to be the young girl in *The Brothers Karamazov*, and everybody laughed, but it turns out that it's a part she might have been able to do. Maybe the simple, uncomplicated Hollywood Hooker thing was just a stage...I mean I think you gotta see growth in *The Misfits*, and she did a better job of comedy in *Hot* than in *Itch*, a much better performance for my money. In the first she just played broadly, in the second she played broadly but she was sweetly believable. Maybe we just got a little more sophisticated in the six or seven years between the movies. And I think back to her time, I really wonder if there would have been better parts for her. I don't think they were making any movies then she could have done any good in. I mean, what was a woman's film in those days? She was going to have to overcome that 'blonde' thing for an awful long time."

I mentioned that you could say that she'd inherited a part from Jean Harlow, and it became her part, and that was what she had to move past. Vic agreed, but he added "The nude calendar -- it was awfully tough to go from the nude calendar to Off-Broadway!"

To Vic, then, Marilyn was strictly an actress, and judged by that, rather than her public persona. And for him she ended up one of the greats. But what would a guy from The Bronx know about Big Blondes?

Joe, on the other hand, born around the same time as Vic, was raised in Brooklyn, spent a lot of time in the street, and a lot more at the Broadway movie palaces. "I was always the first in my group to see what was out because that was in my Broadway cutting days, the early fifties, never going to school, always cutting out, catching every first-run movie. She first entered my horizon in *Asphalt Jungle*. I loved the entire film -- we had a very good eye, this group of us. We should have been used as people they showcased stars on, my bunch of Brooklyn scruffs, because when we saw Marilyn, we knew absolutely she'd be back for many encores. Our cultured brainpans were tuned in somehow.

"There were all sorts of imitators after, but we picked up the special quality...we used to laugh at Mamie Van Doren, looking like the leader of the Tigerettes, that wasn't sexuality. But Monroe had that special thing. Imbued with sexuality but almost mystical. You didn't fantasize. It wasn't that you were going to have her, you just wanted her there to look at. You know, I never thought I could run into her and ball her!

"Now, Bardot, I thought Bardot was absolutely dynamite -- this was five years later, at twenty. To me, for sheer sexuality she came across more than Marilyn, because she was that thing of the super-precocious child inside that woman's body, she knew what she had. Marilyn, though, was innocence to me. I thought she was perfect for *Gentlemen Prefer Blondes*; if I were wooing Monroe I'd have a black opera cape and bonbons and meet her at the stage door. On the other hand, Bardot not only knew absolutely what the game was about, but she could teach you seven ways from Sunday! You felt you had an abyss of sexual ignorance when you looked at Bardot -- and that she knew all about it from the moment when the nuns tried to beat it out of her in that French convent school.

"But, then, I knew there was no sense even fantasizing about Brigitte either, I was so lonely and desperate. I used to fantasize about, God forgive me, some of my friends' better looking mothers...they might invite me in for a glass of Bosco and do something horrible. That seemed accessible. So I didn't lie in bed thinking about either Marilyn or Brigitte.

"I had a wild range to my loves, though. Anna Magnani drove me mad -- she was like the other side of Brigitte. I could never believe, with Monroe, her history that you later knew of how she climbed up on stars and who she balled, I could never believe that she wasn't without that showgirl innocence."

Joe's second love is baseball, so I wondered how he'd reacted to her marriage to Joe D. Because he's been a lifelong National League rooter I might have expected the answer:

"I was depressed when she married him because it reinforced my theory that the Yankees get all the best in life. And then when she married Arthur Miller, then there was hope for all of us who read books and that kind of thing. But I hated that posturing on her. I thought she was a delicious light comedienne, and all this thing of the Russian drama teacher, and the heavy roles, like the one as a psychotic baby sitter, that was a downer for me and the boys. It was like seeing her throw away her natural talents to impress other people -- it was

almost like meeting Willie Mays and finding out he wants to talk about 'Brown vs. the Board of Education! That's not what I want to talk to him about!

"So I think her best films were *Some Like It Hot*, *Gentlemen* and *Let's Make Love*. It must have been a very happy affair with Montand, because she never looked better. The thing with the light comdienne thing is I thought she had a wonderful range there -- even the vignette in *All About Eve* where George Sanders is sending her over to Gregory Ratoff and she says, 'Do they all have to look like bunnies? Like hungry bunnies?' I thought she had a lovely flair. Whereas I thought *The Misfits* was so heavy-laden that if the mustangs saw it first they would have killed themselves!

"Killing...you know, it's odd that I can't pinpoint where I was when she died, or even when I found out she died. Maybe it was just that she was going through all those problems anyway. You heard all those things she was doing on the set, and she was down, so that flavor that once was there was starting to dissipate into a Judy Garland syndrome. But the movies still hold up -- like I said she looks like meringue in *Let's Make Love*."

I wondered about pin-ups, that sort of thing. Joe says they never got into that, that he and his friends focused on certain women in certain films, generally, so that they didn't really exist outside that character. He adds, pumping again for the good taste these kids from Brooklyn had, "It removed it from the sexual a little when I realized that films that certain women looked like dynamite in actually held up as films. I'm thinking of Rita Hayworth in *Gilda*, Ruth Roman in *The Champion*...I think it had a lot to do with the films. I remember, for instance, being grossly disappointed in *Niagara* --and a terrible turkey we crashed in the Roxy to see called *River Of No Return*. That was a real Cinemascope bomb, even with Robert Mitchum."

I had always sort of liked *River*, because I kept waiting for Marilyn and Mitchum to have their eyelids fall down permanently, but Joe felt it was the viewers' eyelids that were waiting to fall. He wanted to talk more about people in films.

"I really think there's a connection when good people know they're working with good material. Not only does their art surface better, but their personality, their sexuality, the whole thing. Contrast Gable in *Gone With The Wind* and Gable in *Parnell*!

"We've seen it in athletes too -- Ali and Frazier brought out the best in each other, while you couldn't believe he was the same Ali as with all those other turkeys he fought. You feel it in yourself when you're really doing something you want to do, as opposed to something that's just a payday. I think mental well-being feeds physical well-being, and physical well-being exudes a kind of energy and sexuality. I think that's what came through in her films.

"It's in the films. That's why I don't have any of her stuff, really, I don't have the calendar, for example. I didn't think she looked that great on the calendar. But she looked great in the movies. And I think the measure of an original is that so many people try to duplicate it...Mansfield, Dors, et al. They were hopeless, they looked like drag queens trying to capture her.

"I was just glad she was there to look at, those wonderful lush and luscious technicolor things. As I've said, I thought she was delicious! I remember one kid in the poolroom who adored her and he used to say...well, I'd rather not quote that.

"And my last word about her is that I think at the end there, when she went through what I call the Russian period, I think all those people worked her over. I think DiMaggio felt the same way, they were taking her where she shouldn't have been. I don't blame Miller for giving it a shot, but when you fall in love you should take people for what they are instead of trying to mold them into an image. I mean she never was Grushenka and she was

never going to reach that place, Dostoevsky, or anything else along that line. I thought Miller should have had the good taste to realize why he pursued her -- George Jean Nathan once listed the reasons that he fell in love, he said 'One of them had a spit curl, and another used to tickle the back of my ear at parties'! He gave a profound and ringing defense proving that these were as good reasons as any ever offered, and I agree with him. Dissecting the logic of love is a fool's game. Because just to find her there in the morning was enough... that's all, for her to lighten up and squeal. She had that child thing, the nice end of it, when she giggled it seemed like there were all sorts of delights there, as opposed to a Bardot, with all her absolute internal knowledge.

"What happens when people let it be is marvellous -- you looked and you said 'It's so natural! She's so gorgeous!' And then when all the pretensions and the problems come in you say 'Oh my God she's into what the rest of us are into!' and the myth starts to erode a little.

"And speaking of the myth, I heard a story about a big star, a comedian, who's very very proud of how he's hung, and he's supposed to have made it with her, and he couldn't understand it two years later when he met her again and she didn't remember him! I thought that was terrific -- not only did she look wonderful, but she gave hope to all us ordinary guys. That's my last word. There's no better gift."

Views From Other Bridges

he magic of the Great Mother is that she appears in so many guises. For the ancients she came as Good Mother, Death Mother, Dancing Mother, Stone Mother. Each was a facet of the mother goddess, each a piece of her, which taken together, formed the whole. Marilyn has this quality, it appears over and over in the talks I've had with a whole range of people. She is attractive to, and attainable for, men and women, straights and gays, young and old. And they all want her for different reasons. Some fantasize, some just want to look at her. Some don't even, they say, react to her sexuality, but to other qualities. Given my own hang-ups I find that hard to believe, but that's my problem.

When Jack Banning mentioned that the bulk of the people he came into contact with at his store were gay, middle-aged, and male, I thought I ought to check that out. Arthur Bell writes a column for *The Village Voice* which deals primarily with show biz, and he also has been an important representative of a gay sensibility for the *Voice* audience, so I started off by asking him some questions. While he says he's not particularly a Monroe fan he had the following thoughts to offer me: "About three or four years ago I was assigned by Esquire to do a piece on Bette Davis, when she was shooting *Burnt Offerings* in San Francisco. She's a very wise woman, you know, and on the second day or so I asked her if she could explain why so many of her fans seemed to be homosexual. She said, 'Yes... they have such good taste!' She said, 'That's why they like me, they like Marilyn Monroe, and they love Barbara Streisand.'

"I thought about it. That's a very good explanation, and it's probably, to some small degree, right. I kind of buy it -- I mean Monroe was beautiful and vulnerable. And I'm sure that at that time in the fifties, when drag was all the rage, as opposed to

the Macho look and checkered shirts and all that now, the gay young men wanted to look like her. They thought that she would be the idealization of themselves. But I don't think that's true now, and I think that if she came along nowadays she'd probably be just as popular with the gay population, except for the Halloween drag balls. I doubt if you'd see any Marilyn Monroe Imitations.

"I remember seeing her in *Niagara* on 42nd Street around 1955, I guess, and the audience was mostly black and mostly tough. They were having the time of their lives when she shimmied down the street. There was a scene -- I still remember it and it was twenty-five years ago, and what was I? Fourteen or so -- and I've never heard such a hullabaloo in a movie house in my life? They just adored her.

"How do I feel about her? I've always enjoyed her in the movies, and just enjoyed her without going absolutely crazy. When her movies were new, I'd always run to see them in the first two or three days after they opened because her movies always meant entertainment with a capital E. I'm talking now about that period from say '53 to '57 when she did *How To Marry A Millionaire, Gentlemen Prefer Blondes* ... they were the equivalent of those big splashy MGM musicals which were adrenalin to us at that point in history. Later on, no, when she did that movie with Yves Montand, that I wasn't too anxious to see, and *The Prince and The Showgirl*, well that one prior to its release had a tremendous publicity campaign so I wanted to see that one a lot. But by the time she had reached about thirty-three or thirty-four, after *Bus Stop*, she became kind of a cliché. I mean, we knew all her tricks, and there was nothing new she could play on us. It was like *Bus Stop* was the definitive movie.

"So as far as her being a gay cult figure, for me, no. At that point I would just as soon have seen someone who was snappy, I would have preferred, say, a Rosalind Russell movie, someone who was a strong kind of 'answer' type woman, to somebody who was cuddly and cutesy, as Marilyn always was.

"Marilyn had a magic she herself didn't know she had— and if she'd known it, she'd probably be alive today! She didn't realize that she was loved by so many people, and if she's in heaven and can look down, I'm sure she's ecstatic."

Even in *Millionaire* I preferred Lauren Bacall to her, in *Gentlemen*, I preferred Jane Russell. But Marilyn was the good straight man, she was Abbott to the Costello of these strong women, and she was a very beautiful Abbott too, and she did her role very very well. That's when I liked her most; in starring vehicles I liked her least.

"Now, *The Misfits* did sort of interest me -- first of all I love horses, I'm sort of an animal lover, so I wanted to see that movie, and I liked her tremendously in it. In fact, except for the musicals that's probably my favorite Marilyn Monroe film. Again I'm going against the grain here. I became a vegetarian for about ten years after I saw that movie!

"One sidelight, here. In '62 I was in Milan, on vacation, and I saw the headlines that Marilyn had died. I just couldn't believe it. The Italian newspapers all had headlines saying I guess *Marilyn Morti* or whatever it is in Italian. It was in a trolleycar, and people were gasping, and I was one of them gasping too. They were literally gasping, and they were hovering over people's shoulders, it was almost like the time when John Kennedy was assassinated in terms of people's reactions.

"I did get her autograph—my interest has always been in movies, not literature or whatever, and I'd seen her in *The Asphalt Jungle* and I used to look for her credits in the movies Fox was making around then, like *As Young As You Feel* and all those. So when I was a kid, I'm going back to '51 or so, I used to collect autographs, and she was in *Monkey Business*. They brought her to New York, to the Roxy I think, for a personal appearance, and she was very, very nice. The kids were interested in her too, because they thought she was going to be a big star. And then later on, probably around '56 or '57, I saw her once or twice again, but she didn't sign. She was a nervous wreck then.

"As far as idealized sexual fantasies about Marilyn, I suppose a gay man could have one, but I suspect that more often it would be someone like

Barbara Stanwyck, or even Gloria Grahame, a strong woman, who kind of represented father. Marilyn represented mother. Does that make any sense? She was like the definitive girl, and for those men who were so inclined, to be that too, she was the one they wanted to imitate. Because with her, you could look like hell, but you'd put on a blond wig, and a corset, and affected the wiggle, and voila! Marilyn Monroe!''

Arthur gave me the names of some people to talk to, gay men who still were interested in Marilyn, and they went into some other areas: her vulnerability, the tragic end of her life, the more predictable stuff. As a matter of fact, while Joe and I were talking about her we had touched on the same area and Joe had said, ''I call it the Garland-Piaf syndrome. I think some gay males make the transference -- they see themselves as tragic heroines manipulated by outside forces, leading dramatic lives at the end. I think that's the appeal with Garland, and with Piaf, and with Monroe. I would not think at the beginning they were into her.''

Of course, from Arthur's comments we see that a great many gay men were into her early in her career, but as a musical comedy star, simply in terms of the big, splashy musicals.

Joe went on, ''If you feel that your true nature is female and you are gay, then you have the persecution of being gay. And when you see a larger-than-life life that's gone through a decline, it becomes kind of a nasty Valentine to the world: *See what you did to me.* I think that's true about most actresses that gay males idealize. I don't think they'd be that interested in a complete, adjusted woman like, say, Simone Signoret.''

I talked to another gay friend. He didn't have much to add, and in fact didn't want to be quoted by name, because he said he was sick of labels. Certainly I can understand that, having been labelled

often enough in my own life. His feeling was that Marilyn, these days, covers the whole sexual range -- that years ago if you liked her you were probably gay, but now it doesn't matter. He said, ''It's like Humphrey Bogart, everybody likes him. Nostalgia's such a big thing now, and Marilyn is a part of that. You can't pinpont who's what by their heroes anymore. Years ago it was different.

''It was different partly because a lot of gay men wanted to look like or be like her.'' Here he was echoing what Arthur had said. Then he added, ''But it may just have been that indefinable star quality she had, which is something gays have always picked up on. Or it could be, of course, the tragic end. And some of them clearly related to her difficult childhood, and to the loneliness. Everybody left her. There's also the whole innocent quality she had, and the softness. That's what makes her different from all the other members of the pantheon, you know, like Streisand and Stanwyck and Crawford and even Garland. And I guess that's why she appeals to everybody regardless of their sexual taste.''

There is always another aspect of Marilyn which keeps intruding into the image of the beautiful Goddess; the unhappiness, the loneliness, the final cop-out. Only one person really wanted to dwell on that, though. Appropriately he's both a poet and involved in a large drug-free rehabilitation project. His name is Frank Lima, and he's been there, and now, working with Phoenix House, he's given a lot of thought to what, in the end, does in people like Marilyn.

''Marilyn first came to my attention when she started going out with Joe DiMaggio. I was about thirteen or fourteen. I was never a baseball fan, but I knew who Joe DiMaggio was, and I discovered she was very attractive, very sexy. I found out she'd been in pin-up magazines, and that made it even better. Then I saw *Gentlemen Prefer Blondes* and I immediately became enamored of her. I thought she was a great looking woman. It wasn't 'til I got older that I realized who she really was, and what she really did. I was very affected by her suicide. Here was an extremely successful woman, and she ended her career like that. I was always curious, given my own problems, about things like that. I believe that part of her whole make-up was that she was addicted to alcohol and pills although she was very successful. She couldn't cope with it, with the success, because she just lacked a lot of other things, like self-esteem. I kind of realize now she couldn't sustain a relationship. It's tragic. There's quite a few of them like that -- Freddie Prinze for instance. I've always been intrigued by that whole thing. Suicide and success, alcohol, pills, drugs. I felt somehow that she managed to live and get healthier -- I felt she was always talented! -- beside being very beautiful, voluptuous, big boobs, all of which became kind of superficial as I got older. I think she would have really broadened her career if she'd gone on. She'd somehow mustered some kind of strength.

"The dramatic thing at the end was the attempt to stretch herself. Of course, I think, in terms of her career, that that would have meant a downhill ride for a while, because she would have become extremely involved in it, and would have done things in imitation of a lot of other people before she integrated it. Then she would have come into her own, she would have incorporated all of that. You know how that is with artists at the beginning --when you want to try something else you become very obsessive, and you do it kind of mechanically, and it really doesn't work out, but then something does happen. You take what you need from those experiences and incorporate it into your own art. But she didn't have -- I hate to use the word fortitude -- but she was unable to continue.

"That's really all I can say. She had no checks and balances at any point. That's how that whole system is set up in Hollywood. "I'm not knocking it. If you have a predilection toward alcohol and other substances, in Hollywood you find people who have the same propensities and who want to help you...that's one of the tragedies in Hollywood itself. I'm not blaming anyone for that or for her. She just happened to be the victim of her own circumstances. Extremely successful, beautiful, talented, however she just didn't have the will to live and go on -- and yet she really worked her ass off! To get all that she got. And then when she did get that, the novelty of working at it was no longer there. And at that point in her life that was a vital point for her survival. The work just wasn't enough to sustain her, and since there was no possibility of a personal relationship, there was nothing left. You try and blot things out.

"I think also that she began to realize her own limitations and who she was, and that became very painful. When some of us are in pain we tend to believe that. People screw their brains out, they drink their asses off, they devote themselves to making money. But in the end you have got to go to bed with yourself.

"I think she was the beginning of a whole era that marked the pulse of America and opportunity. In her case it was very very elegant and publicized, but there's been a lot of others that have done that since. It is a real problem -- not getting political or social about it, but it exists. "It reflects on the

culture and what's going on. It happened to Freddie-boy too. A really talented guy who could have gone on to do a lot of other things too, but again, he had no ego or self-esteem to back up the grandiosity and the accomplishments.

"The point is they were all damaged before they began. Prinze, Marilyn, all of them. She was abandoned, she had no home life, no nurturing. We see that here even with rich kids. The parents give them all the accoutrements of an opulent munificent society, but there's no nuturing. And that's damaging. And you find a way to stop the pain.

"And it's something people don't want to talk about. Especially if they have their own difficulties."

Frank, as I've said, is a poet, and poets have been singing to, and about, the Mother Goddess since the beginning of time. So it wasn't surprising that a very short time after Marilyn's death a collection of poems eulogizing her appeared. What *was* surprising was that the collection came out of the depths of the then East Village, a raunchy collection of post-beats, and soon-to-be hippies, flower children and the like. It was published by, and contained a poem by, Ed Sanders, who later ran the Peace Eye Bookshop, and started a musical group that would become the Fugs. The collection was called, simply, *Poems for Marilyn Monroe.*

"There were these poets, John Keyes, Al Fowler, myself...I guess it was your typical testosterone-maddened '60's chauvinist bar babble that started it. I was into instant printing at the time, so it was done right after she died. That was the real meaning of the mimeograph revolution. It was printed on flaming orange-red Granitex paper which, as I recall, cost a dollar a ream. I got it from the same place The Catholic Worker and other peace organizations got their paper. And it was out within a week or two after she died -- no more than ten days after.

"We all hung out on the Lower East Side, and I probably edited it in Stanley's Bar. My input came, frankly, from *Niagara*, which I'd seen as a very young man. It had terrific effect on my idea of what a divine sexual encounter might be. I don't know how old I was when I saw it -- I knew all about the rudiments of gratification already, because I'd been to Boy Scout Camp where they taught you all those things. I was born in '39, so I was probably 15 or 16, and it had a terrific effect on my sensuality, my sense of feminine pulchritude.

"She was the Magna Mater, the Syrian goddesses, the mommy cults that spewed into later Roman civilization. Later on I was criticized for that kind of feeling by feminist publications, and I can see the point. But at the time it was an honest instant response, it was emotional karate! She died. It was a terrific blow to serious young poets. I think the book was an honest emission of anger, anguish, based on a death that we as young men felt strongly. Please forgive us!

"That was at that point, in the early sixties. It's easy to pule about it later, just like it's easy to fix up your books and your poems ten years later, and to patch up your love life...you'd get a lot more sex in high school if you were there ten years later.

"I didn't have any pin-ups on the wall or anything like that. I guess the photographs in *Eros* must have been later, and that was the only visual input aside from the movies that I ever had. I always depended on mental image -- and occasional pictures in newspapers, I guess. But I never used pictures for the things young men use pictures for. It was a sense of her being something greater than just a blonde mammal. She had a luminous aspect about her!

"Now, you're telling me that a lot of guys you've talked to say she was too much for them to fantasize over? Well, I will go on record as saying I was ready! And if she's on the astral plane, I'm still ready -- and my apologies to my wife. I'm ready to go!

"But I think she may be like James Dean...I mean you really had to be there to get plugged in, and there aren't a whole lot of twelve-year-old James Dean fans. But she had an intellectual apparatus too, she had certain aspects about her, an intelligence. I think she was real smart. She was a listmaker, she got up and she ran her life precisely. She'd get up just like any mogul and make her list. She'd plan out her life in two or three week segments, or a month, and work her way through, and make another plan, which is the way to do it out there. At the least she had a really good sense of what she wanted to do, and she was finely tuned to it. It didn't offend me at all when she started to broaden her reach a little in the later movies. I liked all her movies -- I don't study them though.

"But my response to her is just as good in *The Misfits* as it was in *Niagara*. There's all that nonsense about her causing Gable to get the big one, but I think she was a benign influence on civilization. That was another thing I liked about her and her movies -- I was real concerned, then, about non-violence, passive resistance, the Gandhian Way, Catholic pacifism, and all that, and I thought she fit into that image of human behavior.

"She had no razor-blade edges, no emissions of flame-mouth, she wasn't one of those Hollywood screamers, and yet you got a sense that she was strong, with zero bullshit. She gave off an image of peace. Whether it's true or not, I don't know, but at the time that's the way I perceived it. I don't know quite how to say it...the Greek Goddess of Peace...Irene, that's it. She was Irene, peace!"

Here's some of the poem that Ed wrote for the book. It's been edited a little, both for length, and because Ed felt (apropos of his comments about fixing up your poems later) that some material was just too harsh, looked at from today's perspective, on Marilyn's husbands.

FOR MARILYN MONROE, August 5, 1962

Marilyn is dead   sultry fire sucked back to the brazier
heart gone endless   blotted out in the universe
o you Marilyn . . . .
the hot pills skid with water down yr throat
and sleepy sleepy sleepy the stomach zapping out death
your mind gone on the nod . . . your eyes losing heat and the glaze spreads
out over the cornea   o holy holy tortured human
goddess woman soft like a child i bet o Marilyn dove
of death brought home on the bough   your 2x4 crotch
sapling torn open by the hollywood lightning
yr breasts wd have brought me home as the bottle has brought you
o Marilyn ZAP!   I want to write invective
infect your body with my love and pull you forth to the
genius you bloomed in the gasping
flashes and the scream of Niagara the cocaine flash scorch of Niagara!

Muse of the Theatre Marilyn save be saved yr rotting mind
drugged out by the pills and now zapped out by a
hollywood mortician !   corpse !
Spectre !   out !   You !   to the sunboat !   Anubis gathers in your
Flame !   to the sun !   Elysium !   Home of the rampant !
Solace for the Sexy Dove !   Heart beyond blood and Maya !
Dance you will Marilyn as the dance of Shiva ! . . . .
would that i were in the sky over hollywood
to see the vision
as you entered the Ship of Death and rode out
alone . . . . to have seen you float out over the
cities in the trellis of stars   to have seen
your entry to the Eye of Peace   to have seen your Barge
of love and sensitivity go forth to the rapids
in the petals the blossoms of time, and forth, forever,
your brain a triumph of the end of pain   to have seen
your breasts received in the hot Tides of Desire and
to have seen you winked out in the Splash of Fulfillment !
to have gone with you to Elysium !
over the rivers the lights the creamstream of being
to solace   your buttocks all luster in the
Halls of fulfillment   your arms kissed by the lips of god
which know nothing but understanding,
your mind with the knowing that surpasses !
your heart with the fire that is endless !
your crotch all flame with the myrrh of its glory !
your eyes in death beyond the glaze of your earthly eyes !
your legs are phantom things to wrap around the tree of knowledge
                          who is the man you never had
                                    no never had

o Marilyn !   death is the Starting ! . . . .

©Ed Sanders

It's already been mentioned, and will be again, that Marilyn was non-threatening to women. Every female I talked to commented on this; while not all had been hooked on her, none seemed anxious or jealous or malicious. A particular case in point was the following interview with Emma, an editor in her mid-thirties, raised in the Midwest, and a New Yorker for the last ten years. Sitting with her was a friend a few years older who added a few comments.

"I was sort of a rangy bony tomboyish kid while growing up. I suspect that physical type had something to do with it, but it also had to do with my psychological set. I was permanently molded by seeing *Pat and Mike* and *Desk Set* at an early age, and so, from the time I can remember, Katherine Hepburn was my role model. I had great fantasies about her being my mother -- that she and Spencer had had an affair...and since he was a good Catholic she had had the baby and dropped it in the most out-of-the-way place imaginable, which was, of course, a small town in Iowa. I fantasized that one day we would have a reunion.

"I think that all my young life I very much chose to be like her in the way I wanted to live. To be strong and rangy...to be able to climb a tree, play baseball..."

Emma's friend broke in here to add her feelings on this point: "Her type, busty, a female image with big tits and a hairdo and high-heeled shoes and a certain type of dress -- I could never emulate that. So I just put it in a different category. I never thought about her one way or the other because I couldn't be like her. I didn't want to think about her as the epitome of womanhood!"

Emma agreed, then went on to pursue the psychological aspect, rather than the physical. "Part of the Hepburn thing was a steadfast and heated refusal to be a victim. I think that Marilyn alarmed me as I was growing up because she was so vulnerable and had that sort of liquid-eyed defenselessness. I was a macho kid -- or macha or whatever -- and only now, in my thirties, am I learning to break past those defenses a little and say, 'Excuse me, I feel fucked up tonight,' to my friends, and be able to get a little reassurance. That's been very difficult for me. And there was Marilyn...I think that it was less that I repudiated it intellectually than that it scared me, alarmed me. I suspect she was all the things I've feared about myself and didn't want to admit: the person who couldn't quite make it through the world.

"This is what I'm talking about. I saw quite a few of her movies when I was growing up, and yet they didn't really make an impression on me. But I've re-seen some of them in the last five years, and I'm touched by her performance!

"I wasn't ready to see them earlier. She didn't exist in my hierarchy when I was growing up -- but I suspect now that it was not that I overlooked her, but I rejected her. And in doing that I was rejecting some part of myself. I didn't want to be a little girl in frilly dresses, I wanted to be in jeans climbing a tree...

"I've found that I'm touched by her performances, and not only by the sad, vulnerable parts, but by her humor. That's something I hadn't associated with her. But she was sometimes immensely funny and self-deprecatory in an extremely likeable way."

We talked for a while about how the stereotype of Marilyn is different for everyone, Sex Queen, Comedienne, Sad Victim, Pedestalized Woman, and the like. Emma said what I'd been thinking all along, "I'm sure that's why she's still in our imagination, when lots of other sex symbols have come and gone. She has the power to evoke in a way that most of them don't. I suspect that's because what she projected to the world is malleable, so that different people see different things, make different connections to different parts of her. It's unlike someone who is a straight sex symbol -- whatever that is! -- but who, basically, just bobs around in movies looking busty. There've been plenty of those!"

Emma's friend wanted to add something at this point, which bore not only on this but on what Arthur Bell had been saying to me. Only this was the other side of the coin. "Marilyn was not imitable...I suppose I could decide to do my hair like Brigitte, or act like Marilyn. She had something extra -- and that makes her the subject of fascination. She's like a natural phenomenon -- there's some sort of unique personal charisma. So when you ask how I relate to movie stars, well, there are some I can say, 'I wish I were like her,' or 'if I were the ideal of myself, I'd be like this one,' or, 'she's a completely different type but I can see what's attractive about her,' but Marilyn's just not reachable in that way..."

I couldn't help thinking of the TV docu-drama that had run in the Spring of '80, as part of *Movieola*. They had taken this poor young actress and drilled her so that she walked like Marilyn, talked like Marilyn, dressed like Marilyn, and even looked like Marilyn. And there was nothing there! She not only wasn't Marilyn, but it's almost as if she wasn't even on the screen.

But now Emma was talking about Marilyn's death. "In reading about it now it seems sort of the quintessence of that quality she always carried, sort of 'Excuse me, I don't know whether I can keep things in control, I'm standing awfully close to the edge...' I don't want to make a big deal out of it, but that vulnerability frightened me. It made me want to say 'Toughen up! You can do it!' I know that survivor is a word that's in disfavor, but Marilyn carried around a placard that said, 'Excuse me, but I'm not at all sure I'm a survivor.' That was clearly part of her appeal. And yet I am struck by how evocative she is...and I'm not sure why."

As a partial answer to that wonder on Emma's part, and as one more view from a different bridge, I add a poem from *The Medicine Woman* by Julie Suk.

PIECES

They pulled Jackie from the wax museum
but not Marilyn.
Like the Alabama congressman said,
everything is made for love.

It was an archaeologist named Love
who found a piece of Aphrodite
in a basement storage room.

We all play statues,
waiting to be moved,
melting at the last warmth.

It's *find me, find me,*
complete this form.

published by St. Andrews Press,
Laurinburg, N.C. (©1980)

Posed by MARILYN MONROE

Golden Dreams

Three Different Loves

If you consider the superstars who have grabbed us over the past thirty years— those we thought were superstars, and those who turned out, indeed, to be such —you find differing levels of durability. Elvis still attracts a following, some purely cultic, some a bit macabre. Sinatra moves the over-forties but nobody much else. Brando is now just a good actor. The Beatles are interesting, but more in a historical sense than mythic.

Bogey, Crawford, and the like, all have followings, but no one dreams about them. Marilyn is the only one who still has a magical hold on people. Some see themselves as her long-lost daughter, some build shrines to her, some merely look for her movies whenever they're re-run, and some just have fond memories. But she still exists for almost everyone.

John collects pictures of her. He's thirty-six now, so he was seven or eight when she first began to loom large in the public eye. But he felt the magic even then. "I'd hear my family talk about her. But I didn't know who she was until I went to the movies. I saw *Gentlemen Prefer Blondes* in 1953, the first time I ever saw her. She was very different from anyone I'd known -- my family is all very dark -- and there she was, the blonde hair, the fair complexion. She was just stunning to me.

"But as I saw more of her I realized that her voice, and the way she acted, just didn't relate to the image of her. I mean the pictures on the covers of movie magazines were kind of brassy. But what I saw on the screen was a little girl. The photographs of her were always of a sexpot. So I was intrigued by that difference. And I started collecting those pictures just because I found a magazine with one of her and took it home and clipped it out and saved it. And then I just started saving all of them I could find. So I've been collecting her stuff since I

was eight or nine. It got so that people always associated me with Marilyn; I'd always talk about her movies, about her, about my collection. And every year I'd say, 'I'm getting older, I should stop this nonsense.' When I was twelve I said, 'Well, maybe when I'm sixteen I'll stop.' And at sixteen, of course, I said, 'Well, at eighteen.'

"But the more I saw her, and the more I knew about her, the more I liked her. And I began to read about her. And I began to find out all that stuff, about how she was really a very lonely woman, and a very insecure one, and not really very beautiful either! I mean, she wasn't a classic beauty, not like Ava Gardner, say. And yet she had more than a Gardner or an Elizabeth Taylor — I guess that's what we're talking about, yes? — a quality, an all-together thing, that the others didn't have.

So my collection is, well, pretty much everything that's ever been done on her. Magazine stuff, stills, books, posters. Of course, as far as the movies are concerned, I don't any more go out of my way to see them—I prefer to see them on a large screen rather than television, first of all, and secondly, I've seen them all so much I practically know them line for line.

"At one point, though, I wouldn't miss them on TV. Now, I'll watch TV if I'm home when she's on, but I won't stay home to watch. I'd rather wait 'til the movie comes back to a theater.

"I feel like I know her and I don't know her. For instance, I can draw her, I know where her hair falls, how her body is, and yet, of course, I don't know her at all. When I was a kid I wrote to her, I was about sixteen. It was when she was living in New York about a year before she died. I said, 'I don't like reading about you in the hospitals all the time. I hope I don't have to read that any more...' I didn't want to have to read the words, 'she died.' About a month and a half later I got a photo of her, but no answer to the letter itself. Of course I didn't really expect that, all I'd asked for was a picture.

"I saw her only once in person. I remember waiting for two hours, with my father, at the premiere of *Some Like It Hot*. It was very cold and we waited and waited. She finally turned up and it was sensa-

tional -- people were being knocked down to get a look at her. And I never saw anyone so white in my life. She had the whitest hair, she was like a ghost, a vision. She was at the peak of glamor. I'm sure if I had seen her the next day, shopping say, I wouldn't have been as satisfied. Oh, I would have been thrilled to see her, but it wouldn't have been the same as this.

"It's hard for me to say what my 'favorite' movie is. I thought her best performance was in *Bus Stop*, but the first two I saw sort of stick with me: *Gentlemen Prefer Blondes,* and *How To Marry A Millionaire*. It's sort of like first love, I guess, since I was so young when I saw them and they were so magical.

"If I had to pick a scene, though, I know which one it would be. It's in *Bus Stop,* and she's with the girl and they're on the bus, and she's talking, she's telling the girl what kind of man she would marry. She's saying it in a very sensitive way, and it's just a beautiful scene.

"I saw her as an actress then, and I saw her sensitivity, and I saw her as a real person. I felt that when she was reading those lines she felt very strongly about them...As far as her as a dramatic actress, I couldn't wait for that day to come, and I was sorry it had to be in *The Misfits*. I just didn't like what Miller wrote there. But I couldn't wait for her to win an Oscar -- I knew that she would, some day. In *Bus Stop* she deserved at least a nomination, maybe not the Oscar, but at least a nomination, and they didn't give it to her.

"Listen, I think she would have been good in *The Brothers Karamazov*. I know they wanted her for the role, and something happened so that she couldn't do it, and Maria Schell did it. But I wanted to see her in it. I remember wanting to see *River Of No Return* just because it wasn't a musical and it wasn't a comedy. Unfortunately it was just a bad movie.

"I felt like, if they gave her the right part she could have done anything. If she were around today? I don't think she'd be making too many films. I think she'd be very selective. I think she'd probably have a Dietrich kind of thing in Vegas. You know, appearing in very glamorous outfits and singing a few songs and talking. And I think she'd be doing a

"She was the last beautiful woman in her culture allowed to have a belly! They even dressed her in a way that would make it seem bigger!"

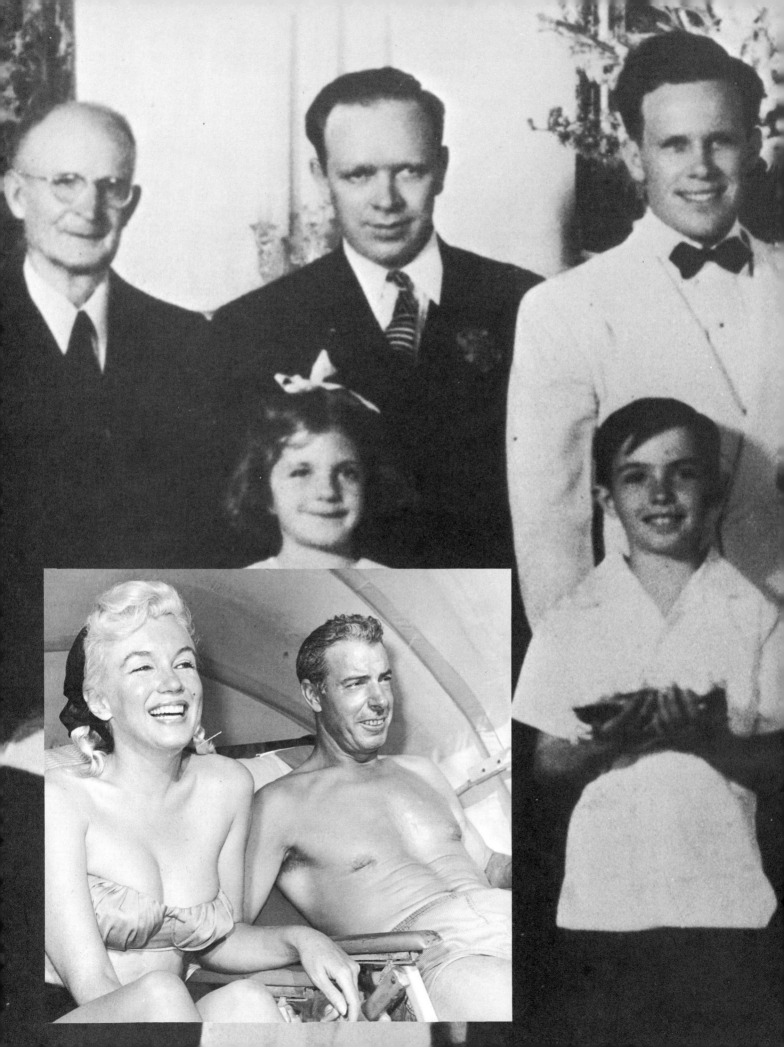

few carefully picked movies.

"I think if she'd been at MGM, say, instead of Twentieth Century Fox, you would have seen her differently. I think they would have made a 'lady' out of her instead of just a sex-pot. I think she would've been given different roles.

"But I have to say that to me she was sexy-looking but not sexual. I never thought of her as a sexual person, although I knew she was sexy-looking. I remember years ago reading a comparison between her and Brigitte Bardot. It said, 'Brigitte is the kind of person you fantasize about and then you go out and find her, and Marilyn you only fantasize about. You can't take her home.'

"Marilyn had a magic she herself didn't know she had -- and if she'd known it, she'd probably be alive today! She didn't realize that she was loved by so many people, and if she's in heaven and can look down, I'm sure she's ecstatic. I'm sure the people at Twentieth Century, the ones that were there then, were surprised after her death -- and now -- that she still lives on."

Most people weren't or aren't collectors, they don't have the special interest that John does. Karen, who's in her middle thirties, is a writer, and editor, and, like many women her age, has been deeply involved in the feminist movement for the last decade. I'd already heard several woman talk about how non-threatening Marilyn was to women and I thought it would be interesting to ask Karen about that, from the 'political' viewpoint. But I found more there, since Karen also had been deeply affected by Ms. Monroe.

"Movie stars and people like that didn't generally move me very much. I didn't have, once I was beyond the age of twelve or thirteen, stars that I attached big feelings to. And I never particularly thought of myself as a fan, at least in the sense of collecting pictures or anything like that. I grew up on a farm until I was twelve, when we moved to the city, and that really makes a difference. When you live on a farm you don't get to the movies very often, and your various passions and interests tend to be very private.

"So my first clear memories of her are when I was young adolescent -- say, starting in '56 or so. I liked her because she was so funny and so soft. That was wonderful -- to know a woman who was both of those things! She had that cotton candy for hair, and that soft, soft face and soft, round body, and her funny little breathy voice. From a child's perspective that could be seen as childish, and looking at clips of her now she was indeed quite babyish sometimes. And she also was a bit Martian! It was like she came from somewhere else where they talked differently than us, and you suspected there probably weren't very many of her people! She had that 'stranger in strange land' quality, and I think that was part of her fascination.

"And I remember having different awarenesses of her, so that she was different images at different times. The most common perception of her seems to be as utterly pathetic -- and that's the one that I'm most uncomfortable with. I've always found it condescending...

"What I'm saying is that when I was little she was this soft, funny lady, and I had a great crush on her, and thought she was wonderful. I remember seeing *Gentlemen Prefer Blondes* -- it's the first movie I remember seeing, so it made a very vivid impression on me. I can remember tooling around singing 'a kiss on the hand may be quite continental...' That's part of how she was funny for me, and why it was hard for me, later, to see her as pathetic. There was real wit in that soft lady singing that tough song; and, also, there she was in contrast to Jane Russell, who was the other kind of bad lady. Russell was real tough, and had breasts like rockets, and all that stuff.

"I found Russell fascinating, too, but in a different way. I guess I found all big-breasted women fascinating, just as I was fascinated by the prospect of my own. So I tended not to be threatened. In fact, it was great, it made them both so vivid, such a presence, and they both played on it, of course."

Since we were talking about the reactions of a young soon-to-be woman, I asked Karen how she felt about other reigning beauties of that day, people like Brigitte Bardot, Elizabeth Taylor, and so on. She said she saw Brigitte for the first time at a forbidden drive-in movie when she was fifteen or sixteen. "I thought she had the most beautiful body I'd ever seen, and I think that's true to this day. She's exquisite. Elizabeth Taylor was really very different for me, because she started as this gorgeous child actress. I never found her sexy the way these other women were. She wasn't packaged that way; it wasn't her role. I thought she was very beautiful, but I wasn't ever particularly interested in her."

Strangely, this had been true for me also. Maybe it was my nascent fascination for blonde goddesses, maybe Elizabeth was too much for my limited self-image at that time, but I also couldn't get in-

terested in Liz. Later, when she married Mike Todd, I used to say that she was too Jewish-looking for me -- and that might have been it, actually, what with the dark, intense beauty she had. My feeling was that the goyim could fantasize about her, but I was perfectly happy with Marilyn.

Karen agreed. "Of all the actresses I looked at and thought about then Marilyn was the most evocative, the only one who really captured my imagination. And then at some point I saw a photograph -- which I sneaked out from under my older brother's bed -- and it was the famous calendar shot. I remember looking at the magazine picture -- and remember that it was a great sin for me to have gone, consciously, and taken it, since we were Catholic -- and quivering with excitement, trying to learn things!

"It was startling to come across her in that context...it was a bad book, full of wickedness, and there was my wonderful soft, funny lady off doing other things! But, I remember, I knew somehow from the beginning why she'd had the picture taken, that she did it for money, was down on her luck, was struggling, all that. I had very mixed feelings, though, because I certainly liked being able to see her full body uncovered. That's always interesting with somebody you know, and I felt I knew her by then. But I also felt indignant that she ever had to suffer, that she could be taken advantage of that way. The other two things I remember thinking are first, that she was skinnier than I thought, and then that they'd done this funny thing, putting her on her side, so that her breasts had gone all funny shapes!

"I don't think you'd ever again find a *Playboy* photograph that was posed like that. The breasts tend to lengthen and flatten out in a most peculiar way, they tend not to look sexy, but teat-like. Remember, I was looking at it with a critical thirteen-year-old eye, female no less, and I thought, 'She's far more wonderful than that. Aren't they stupid -- they think they can get her by making her lie down naked and taking photographs of her!' So I was indignant that she could ever have been so hungry that she'd had to do this thing, but they didn't get her anyway! It made it seem as though the photograph wasn't even an exposure of her."

I felt constrained at this point to tell Karen that even in this breast-crazy America, some of us saw past *Playboy* and its "ideals." As I've noted before, I do indeed like breasts -- indeed I find them magical -- but I've never had a need for either size or specific shape. I suppose the mere baring of a breast is enough, given my deprived childhood.

And then, flat or full, firm or sagging, it's exciting. But what strikes me, these days, looking at the calendar, is that Marilyn's breasts are not huge, not compared to the anatomical freaks we've been subjected to constantly since the invention of silicone implants.

Karen wanted to return to an earlier remark. She said, "I think it's very important about Marilyn in respect to other women. I mean about the skinniness. I didn't realize then that her figure fluctuated so much, and that later in her career she was heavier than other glamorous women. But the point here was that her figure was almost girlish, and I was just beginning to be girlish myself, so I was curious about it. It was almost as if for the first time I realized we inhabited the same continuum, so that what had been originally almost a daughter's reaction to her was now a younger sister's.

"The images after that are pretty much discrete. I didn't particularly follow her or her career -- as a teenager I was atrocious about reading newspapers and since we had very strict rules about television in the house, I just didn't see a lot of news. I don't remember much about her thing with DiMaggio, any of that. I sort of jump to the famous shot of the skirt blowing up from *Seven Year Itch*. There she was! She was my pretty lady again, shapely and soft, and the picture's comical. It's a wonderful photograph, and I still love it.

"And the next time around is a clutch of memories of her in *The Misfits*, and things going bad for her. I might have seen photos in *Life* or *Look* and if I did, I would have looked at them, but none of them made any impression on me. So *The Misfits* and the movie she made with Yves Montand --*Let's Make Love* -- I saw those. I remember being aware in *Let's Make Love* -- here we go again about the body -- that she was really quite plump. She wears

"Later, when I had all sorts of sophisticated adult thoughts about her, and esthetically oriented ones at that, and considered her from a feminist perspective, I realized that was why I found her such an appealing female image -- that she did have that full, slightly sloppy, incredibly human body. That accorded with my notion of how women really are, that they spill over and they leak and they're real. It stood in terrific contrast to all those idealized slender nearly amputated women who were beginning to become popular. You know, the Russells and the Mansfields gave way to the Twiggys. If you look back to the late sixties, just before that began, if you look at say Jean Shrimpton, who was Girl of the Year, you'll be surprised at how big she was, what hips and thighs she had. She was really substantial. Then this whole 'androgynous' thing took off with Twiggy, which I think was half positive and half hostile, and a body like Marilyn's was suddenly out of it."

Karen and I shifted from this 'body language' to the films themselves, but I was glad she'd talked about it. I remember for myself, how much my own views of women, growing up in a mostly male household, were formed by movie images. As a pre-teenager, I'd been terrifed by Mae West -- she was so brassy, so hard, and so raucous in her humor. And I'd been totally knocked out at thirteen or fourteen by the famous wartime cheesecake shot of Rita Hayworth kneeling on a bed. I suppose my kids will end up formed in the same way by Bo Derek and Suzanne Sommers and the rest. And I suspect Karen is right in finding Marilyn the healthiest image of the bunch. But, on to the movies...

"My favorites were *Gentlemen*, *Some Like It Hot*, and *The Misfits*. Despite all the criticism of *Misfits* I thought it was a wonderful movie, and that it brought her out as a serious actress in a way that nothing else had. I thought she had genuine acting talent, and her use of her body as an acting instrument is just terrific. There's the scene where she walks into the bar and they all look at her ass, and there's the eeriest scene in the movie, the long shot in the desert where she is contorted. I'll never forget that pose: knees together, legs splayed out, all squeezed down, and then her arms come out and she screams 'Murderers!' It's probably the only time she was ever filmed raising her voice! She's in a helpless rage, and that's chilling to see how, because it was her chance to turn on the culture that produced her, and name it."

those gathered gowns in that movie that emphasize the plumpness, and I always loved that about her, that she could be heavier than other women and still be regarded as such an ideal!

I remembered being very unhappy with the end of the movie, from a writer's viewpoint. As a young poet, of course I thought I could write better than anybody alive, and it seemed to me that Miller had

copped out on the finish of the film. I don't know how I would've ended it myself, or at least I can't remember, but I do remember that I thought he'd sold the story short, gone for an easy way out. Now I see that what I was upset about was his reaction to his and Marilyn's own scene -- just as Karen was reading Marilyn's response to the culture around her into it. We were both probably right, too. At that point in our viewing the movie had nothing to do with it, we were seeing life. That's always dangerous when what you're supposed to be doing is being entertained, except where art is concerned, so maybe both Marilyn and Miller did better than we knew.

But now Karen wanted to talk more about those external forces she had felt. "When I said before that I was irritated by the stuff about her being pathetic it was because I think that's an extension of the cultural attitudes that ground her down. She was, of course, a victim of her culture, and also, of course, she collaborated in her own destruction. And in real life terms she was just a wretchedly unhappy person who was more bent on doing herself in than not.

"Recently I read some excerpts from that tell-all book her housekeeper wrote, or rather I skimmed some excerpts. And I found I didn't want to go on and read the book, it was just depressing, depressing in that grimy way where you think you're not even going to learn anything through the grime! If it was an accurate account, then she was, on a private, day-to-day level, destructive in that ordinary familiar way that people often are, and I just wasn't interested."

Of course, I said to Karen, it's just on that day-to-day level that you can learn something -- if it isn't done grimily, isn't done just to shock. Demythologizing the 'great' often makes them greater. Shakespeare becomes more when we find out he was married to a shrew, Melville forced to crank out a living in the Customs office makes us more aware of the real miracle Moby Dick was. But the "inside stuff" too often does turn out nonsense, and as she said, merely depressing.

And Karen wasn't depressed by Marilyn, rather she was inspired. "I've never gotten over the idea that she died because she was basically a good person! I had a sense that her end was one possible conclusion to being the perfectly accommodating woman...she was rewarded for that by being elevated, magnified -- but in the end, if you're not secretly really tough it just does you in, because no one can be only an accommodation. I've always linked her with Jacqueline Kennedy in my mind, because I see them as the two poles of a single ex-

perience: the woman who really plays ball with her culture. At one end we have the winner, Jackie Onassis -- I wouldn't want what she's won, but at least you can see what you can do with it, that is, marry Onassis and hope he dies -- and at the other end Marilyn. Marilyn, who I imagine kept trying actually to be loved for herself!"

I started having visions of a play revolving around Marilyn and Jackie and Jack, one in which Marilyn *is* loved for herself, by Jack, and where Jackie is gaining the rewards for her accommodation. It would make a hell of a script, I said to Karen! Unfortunately it would probably just get turned into another version of *As The World Turns*. But this problem of being loved for one's self is universal, and not limited to "sex goddesses." And we all do go on accommodating ourselves to the world, and then wondering why no one sees the real us! Did Karen think she was that much of an innocent about the way the world works?

"I don't think," she said, "that the way she ends makes her a pathetic figure, because I don't think she went into show business blindly. I think it's quite possible she posed for the calendar when she wasn't, in fact, starving to death, but was just trying to make her way in the world. That deck was surely stacked, but she did collaborate in it, and she made herself, as I said, accommodating...she *was* accommodating, those great milky breasts saying 'Come on, everybody, let's eat!' I think when you're that way, that much, some men want to kill you. Not all men, obviously, but some. It's that basic cultural thing that she was and that she tapped and that she was shaped into. All kinds of men wanted to do all sorts of things to her -- God knows what Miller wanted to do, maybe make her read the Syntopticon or the Great Books!

"Of all the men, DiMaggio was probably the most innocent. But they were still an incredibly iconic couple -- as were she and Miller. I think she had an instinct for that, that she also lived, sometimes, on the iconic level. But this thing about men wanting to kill you when you're accommodating, in a sense it's true, it's behind all that snuff porn, the close connection between sex and death. And I do think the sexes are at war, profoundly and terribly tangled. There's a real problem there and has been since before history began: men coming to terms with women as reproductive beings, and as their mothers. Women are, literally, the spaces men come out of! And sure, Marilyn was form of the Mother Goddess. It's that simple. Except that it's anything but that simple..."

Sitting in Karen's office, talking about the complexity of that "war," I thought about an in-

teresting theory I'd run across in Barry Fell's *America B.C.* He's talking about the various monumental sculpture left by early man, and he gets off into a sidetrack about "blood sacrifice," a favorite subject of archaeologists and the common man. And he posits that the little grooved cup-like indentations found at a lot of worship sites might not be for collecting the blood of the victim at all, but just might be for taking the semen of the male worshippers. It makes good sense, if you're serving a Mother Goddess to give proof of your potency --but men seem to find it much easier to think in terms of killing. So Karen's thoughts about snuff porn and bloodlust aren't off the mark at all, strong as they may sound. And it isn't only in obscene books and movies that the feelings crop up either, as Karen's next comments show.

"Recently I saw a documentary about her on television and it had a lot of clips in it I'd never seen. I'll tell you what I remember most from it --her singing Happy Birthday to President Kennedy. I'd seen stills of that, but not the actual footage, and it's quite something to watch, because it's the only image of her I've ever seen in which there is really an element of self-abasement. It's very disturbing, that bit of film, and I had expected to be charmed by it...Then there were clips of her after the divorce from Miller, when she was so miserable. Her lawyer is bringing her out of divorce court and the reporters are leaping on her like hounds. She was just so shattered, she was falling apart, and they kept going at her. At one point her lawyer puts his arm around her to steady her, and she turns toward them and actually tries to answer! And then it comes over her, or so it seems, how appalling it is, and she stops and she says something like 'Please, please, get me out of here...' and the lawyer hustles her into the car and off, with the newsmen still bashing at the windows. It's hideous, it's as if they wanted to eat her alive!"

I've seen that clip too, and Karen is right, it is hideous. But of course, as I told her, and as she well knew, that hunger was at least partially caused by our hunger. That's how you sell newspapers and how you get an audience for television. We keep wanting to bite into those people we see as stars, to take a piece of them to strengthen ourselves, even if it's by saying "See, she's rich and famous and beautiful and she's still miserable just like me!" It's one reason why I hardly ever do "real" reporting for my column in the *Voice*, because I don't want to chew over some poor bastard who's in trouble. So I tend to sit back and comment -- read: re-act -- on the foibles of time. I call it contemplative reportage, as opposed to the more infamous investigative stuff.

But we'd talked a little about Marilyn's accommodation, and implicit in that was the exploitation of that body of hers. Did Karen want to comment a little on that? The answer was a little different than I'd expected.

"I don't want to keep harping on the body thing, but she was the last beautiful woman in her culture allowed to have a belly! They even dressed her in a way that would make it seem bigger. And she was also allowed to have real breasts! In the later movies they were far from ideal, they were fat, they fell about, they showed the age she was. And she was put in dresses with no bras, and nothing else like that existed. I think it's true that people didn't even know she was a Mother Goddess. They just called her a sex symbol...but the profoundest sex symbol had better be a Mother Goddess, or you're just not getting at the bottom of things. And that's another reason too why she wasn't a pathetic figure. Mother Goddesses never are. They're fertile and you may not be.

And, of course, I added, men can't be. You can be potent, sure, but how will you know unless you make the Mother pregnant? And even then, as the poets never tire of telling us, you don't even know if it's you that's potent!

"One of the loveliest things," Karen said, "about her was that she was accessible to women. The culture kept telling us she was the ultimate sex symbol, the blonde bombshell, and they bleached her hair 'til it was snowy white, and gave her perfect lipstick, and made her chic. And she was still accessible to women! I never felt excluded by her, not when I was little, not when I was older. I think my responses to her were every girl's responses to her mother. Who wouldn't want to be cuddled in those breasts, and climb back inside that nice warm belly?

"Back in the early seventies when a lot of us in the woman's movement started consciousness raising, and doing research, and trying to look at our culture from this new perspective, one thing we talked about a great deal was different idealized images of women. And Marilyn was always a very sympathetic figure for us. Oh, there were unimaginative women who said, 'Yes, a lot of cleavage, and painted and stuck up like a doll,' instead of seeing her complexity as a cultural image, as a person who became an icon. But there are unimaginative, one-dimensional people everywhere. And I never heard a woman bad-mouth her!

"The unimaginative reactions to her -- the condescending notion that she was 'destroyed,' 'pathetic,' -- they render her unreal, totally passive. I

think she was almost active in her passivity. She was so so nice -- and I don't know one woman who won't admit that sometime in her life she wanted more than anything just to please. That's part of how women are trained from the time they are babies. Two and three year old girls by and large try harder to please than two and three year old boys. The question, of course, is to please whom? Everybody and anybody! And that quality was so intensified in Marilyn, as with the reporters, when for a minute, while they were ripping her to pieces, she still tried to give them what they wanted! I think it's conceivable that she suspected this lethal element in her relationship to the culture.

"And it's extraordinary to think when we talk about this image of her as Mother Goddess, that death should be so much a part of it. Because it really isn't possible to think of her as growing old; it isn't possible to imagine her surviving without changing a great deal. And she didn't make the change. I think she may have been trying to.

"I can only speculate how or whether she thought about any of this stuff. But it's reasonable to guess that she came to feel trapped, terrified -- and hooked on her iconic image! That's enormously seductive, and particularly for someone whose inner resources were as shaky as hers. If it bent Dylan out of shape, why wouldn't it do it to Marilyn Monroe? Being a superstar is a grotesque experience and potentially very deforming. It has to be worked with all the time or it's unmanageable. And she was the ultimate superstar!"

That led us back to Marilyn herself, what *made* her the ultimate superstar. "She was genuinely resonant as a person. It's interesting to look at someone like Jayne Mansfield. She didn't have as pretty a face, but it was all right, and she certainly had the fabulous giant body, the blonde hair, and all of that -- and, of course, the gap between them is infinite! Marilyn had a powerful inner reality, and she could bring some of it to acting. I've never understood how anybody could think she was a bad actress -- I've seen her to be too good in too many things, and the pictures really hold up. A lot of people don't understand movie acting. It's just as hard as stage acting, it's just totally different. She was really a good movie actress, and revolutionary in an Arthur Miller play, but then what a silly waste! There's a limit to casting against type..."

Karen and I talked a little about how badly Hollywood has used that notion -- which is essentially a good one. To cast against type can sometimes make a startling difference in a movie. But unfortunately usually it just means another hype. What might have been wonderful would have been to be able to see what kind of roles Marilyn would pick for herself were she still alive. She'd have the power to do that now, and she might have surprised us all. But Hollywood's notion would, in fact, have ended up with her being that intellectual revolutionary, and falling flat on her face at it.

And, speaking of type, I asked Karen if she felt Marilyn fell into any particular stereotype as a person who was a star. Did Karen find her image off-screen banal or trite?

"What strikes me now about Marilyn is how little she hurt people, given how unhappy, screwed up, disorganized she was. She really didn't seem to have a mean bone in her body, which is not to say she couldn't be selfish and drive people crazy and all, but that's different. I'd really be surprised if it turned out she had a ferocious, aggressive, malicious personality that had somehow managed to never come out. It never comes as a surprise to me that she was self-centered, like all show business people; the surprise is when you encounter an actor or actress who isn't.''

What's more surprising about that to me is that people accepted her so readily -- I'm not talking about the people she had to work with whom she did drive crazy -- but the fans. No matter what she did, it became what they expected her to have done. This theme recurs over and over again, in these interviews, and whenever I talk to people about her, or about theater people in general. They bring her name up even when we're talking about others. But Karen remembered a particular case that did involve other show people.

"Simone Signoret has a thing in her book about when Montand and Monroe had their affair while they were making *Let's Make Love*. Signoret is something of a Mother Goddess in her own right of course, and she saw it all happening, saw Marilyn getting him. She and Montand seem to have one of those marriages that was made in heaven -- they've been together since the year one -- and she seemed to be counting on that to help her see it through. But my memory of her is that she said, 'I didn't blame her. She couldn't help it! She just had to do it!' It was like blaming the sea for knocking over a sand castle...and that's what I think of when I hear about her making a list of icons she wants to sleep with.

"There's this infinite naivete, a streak of 'Maybe I'll find it just around the corner. Maybe it will be with him!'

She's a little bit like a character out of *The Wizard of Oz*, going to get a heart from DiMaggio, brains from Arthur Miller...But I don't think she had any real armor, because real armor isn't on the outside, and she was a kind of mess on the inside.

"Listen, I realize that I'm still mad about her being dead! I was mad then, and I'm mad now. It was a waste, and we should all be somewhat ashamed."

This stuff from Karen was so good, so strong, that after we finished talking, I said to myself, "That's it. That's the definitive interview." And in many ways it is. But then I met Lenny, and I decided there were two definitive interviews, because Lenny is just as good and just as strong, and he's coming from a man's viewpoint.

Lenny is in his early forties, a playwright who's done some work in the movies, and some on New York's off-off Broadway stages, so he's had a wide range of experience with people in show business. And I suppose I was surprised to hear that he loved Marilyn, because playwrights learn early to distrust actors and actresses. But I forgot that playwrights, like poets, have something deep inside that draws them to the magic around special people, that lets them see beyond the stereotype or the image.

Lenny also seemed to draw 'Marilyn-people' to him, as did many I talked to, particularly after I asked them to think about their feelings about her. He was on his way downtown to meet me and my tape recorder, sitting in the subway, when a very buxom blond girl came in and sat down across from him. Three East Indians came in with her and sat down next to him. They seemed, he says, to be separate from her -- a middle-aged man, a young man, and a boy.

"Everyone is rocking and rolling along in the subway, when the blonde cranes her neck, as if looking at a car card. She is. It's a Bowery Savings Bank ad with Joe DiMaggio in it. She looked at me, and then at the three Indian guys, and she says, 'Did you know he was married to Marilyn Monroe?' Well, at first I thought she was just the usual subway crazy, and then I realized she was with them, and just passing on information. But can you imagine? Coming down here to meet you to talk about Marilyn, and there she is on the subway! Marilyn is going to go on forever!

"For me, I first became aware of her in the army. It was maybe '56, '57, and there was a big thing about her in the army. But, also, I was stationed in Europe, France and Germany, and she had come over to England to do *The Prince and The Showgirl* with Olivier, so there was a lot of publici-

ty about her. I remember particularly because Olivier was my favorite living actor, next to Brando, so I was excited about the film -- although most of my friends kept saying 'It's not going to be any good, it's not the kind of film we've seen her in.' They were talking about things like *Niagara*, which was playing on the base a lot then, and which they loved. I remember seeing *Niagara* in Rome, on a leave. I'd already seen it in America and now I saw it dubbed. Everybody there loved it - when she walked in in that red dress they all went 'Bravissima! Bravissima!' And her pictures were all over Paris, even little towns like Verdun.

"But wait, I just thought of something -- actually the first time for me was college, before the army. I went to a small Catholic college -- we were all aware of her of course, but the first time I paid any real attention was in an English Lit class. We'd walked in and on the blackboard it said 'Marilyn Monroe for President,' so it had to be the '56 campaign. The teacher was a priest, and he just looked at it and laughed but didn't erase it. My next class was in the same room and when I came back in someone had crossed the line off and written 'What would we do with a bitch for president!, and had underlined the 'bitch' several times and drawn a dog next to it!

"I can't think of anyone who didn't like her, college or army, except that guy who wrote on the blackboard. There were pinups of her all over college and the army, and, of course, the movies. She was a big thing to all of us.

"I was a movie freak then, the theater thing didn't start 'til after the army, so I saw everything. And then, later, I saw her! I never met her, and I wish to hell I had, but one day I did get to watch a beautiful scene with her. She was standing in front of the Plaza Hotel, it was while she was married to Miller, it was in June, and she was in a white dress. She was all white! The skin, the hair, the dress --the only thing not was the red lips! I've seen a lot of movie stars. I wrote a movie for Sophia Loren and I got to know her well, I've known Faye Dunaway for a long time...but Marilyn, for me she was the most breathtaking woman of all.

"I'll never forget this scene, either. She was posing for pictures for *Look* magazine. She took off her white shoes, the high heels, with everybody standing around and the photographers waiting, and a limousine waiting for her too, and she waded in the pool and waved at us, filled her shoe up with water and threw it out at us...I couldn't believe how she looked, so happy, so beautiful...and I looked at all the people gathered around, every type, and they were all enchanted. I remember one woman saying to the man with her, 'Isn't she lovely! What would you do with her?' And he said, 'I'd just put her on a shelf and look at her for the rest of my life!'

"I wouldn't have just looked at her, but I knew what he meant. I used to fantasize about her in bed -- I guess everybody did -- but I would pretend the pillow was her and I would talk to it, you know, get into it slowly. With someone like Brigitte I'd start right off, but with Marilyn I'd have to build up...I'd say things like, 'You're like a little baby, you're beautiful...' and she'd say, 'I'm not such a little baby! Why don't you try me?'

"Well, I'd build the whole thing up. And the fantasies kept up, too. They got better when she married Miller, because by then, you know, I was writing plays myself, and I thought, 'Well now, that's pretty good -- she married a playwright!' The sexual thing was always there. When I saw her sing for Jack Kennedy at the Garden I freaked out. She was wonderful. And every time I saw her on television, or in the news, I kept saying, 'I can't believe this, I can't believe her, she's so beautiful.'

"I'll tell you something. That day in front of the Plaza was really kind of wonderful because she was the most glowing movie star I've ever seen. She was bigger than life...and loving every minute of it. I remember she put her shoes back on when she was all finished with the pictures and she blew kisses at

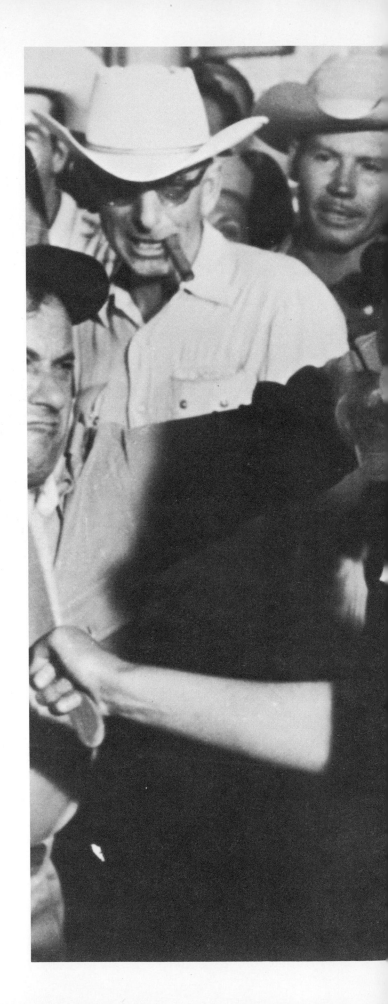

everybody. We all applauded her, and there wasn't one unkind thing said, one unkind look. I'm not kidding. The vibrations she gave out came across. Listen, just the other day, I was on an Eighth Avenue bus and we passed a store with posters of her in the window. And this old couple, an old Jewish man and woman, saw the window, and the woman said, 'Oh, wasn't she a beautiful woman, isn't it a shame?', and the man said, 'We miss her, don't we? She'll never make any more movies...'

Since Lenny is a playwright I asked him how he felt about Marilyn as an actress and not as his great love. "One thing I really loved about her was that she did try to act -- when she didn't have to! She made a genuine and sincere attempt at acting, and she already had her own thing going. I mean as a comedienne. Yet she did want to *act*, so she almost had to get involved with Strasberg and the Actors Studio and Arthur Miller and all. She had no choice. They all represented what she wanted so she had to do it. But I guess in a way I wish she hadn't tried...

"I loved her in *The Misfits* and I knew she couldn't have done that movie without all the other stuff. But still, well, let me tell you something else I remember. It wasn't too long after The Plaza, and I was standing in the rain for the opening of *The Misfits*. I think it was at the Capitol Theater -- I think *The Misfits* was the last picture they showed -- and a friend and I were waiting in line. And it was a huge line, to see Marilyn. Oh, sure, to see Gable and Clift *and* Marilyn, but really to see Marilyn. All of a sudden this little green limousine, a little foreign one with a chauffeur, pulls up where the line was. Strasberg had his Senior Dramatic Workshop classes in a studio above the Capitol --the Actors' Studio wasn't there, but these classes were -- and, anyhow, the chauffeur gets out and comes around and opens the door. Lee Strasberg --I'd met him so I knew what he looked like -- gets out, and he and the chauffeur are standing there with little umbrellas, and Marilyn gets out!

"Here's this huge line waiting in the rain to see her in a movie, and she's getting out of a car! She had a babushka over her hair, and low heels, and huge hornrim sunglasses, and she was trembling, and she could hardly walk. And Strasberg and the chauffeur broke the line so they could all go upstairs. But she never even noticed the line because she was trembling. And it wasn't too long after this that she did herself in."

I knew that Lenny had once had a signed picture from Marilyn, one that was a little special, because a friend who'd worked with him in the old days had told me. I asked him about that story. "It was

right after the Plaza Hotel thing. I went home and wrote a piece of fiction, but it was a letter, written sort of like a short story. It's from this guy who's a sixteen year old Cuban living in the U.S. You know, the whole thing with Castro was going on then...and the idea in the piece was maybe she could save the world if the me in the story, Oswaldo Fernandez was his name, had a chance to marry her! And he, I, asks if she can write him, me, so he, I, can show it to his, my, friends. I showed it to everyone, everyone loved it. I would read it out loud to people, even. It's about harmony, how she could make the world harmonious. Then I decided to send it around, you know, submit it for publication. I sent it to The *Village Voice*, The *New Yorker*, *Esquire*, everywhere. It was rejected all over! But I always got nice notes with the rejections...you know, they have those printed cards, but when they add something in handwriting you think they may be serious. And they all said, 'Try again!' It got the best reaction of anything I'd sent around 'til then.

"Well, I had a friend at that time who was studying with Lee Strasberg, and he was doing a scene with her, the park bench scene from *Golden Boy*. He'd read the thing and he said, 'Lenny, send it. Send it to her now. Tell her you're a playwright and send it to her. She'll love it!' And, of course, he had her address -- he used to work with her up in the apartment, he'd drive me crazy describing everything in it -- so I sent it to her with a little note. I just said that I was trying to get it published but that that didn't matter, I just wanted her to see it because she had inspired it. And about a week later I got a manila envelope and there's a picture of her that's so beautiful you couldn't believe it! And it's inscribed to me from her, and there's also a little note attached, and she says, 'This is my favorite picture ever taken of me' -- it's the one by Cecil Beaton where she's lying on a sheet with flowers -- 'I only send it to certain people, and I think you should have it after what you did for me in your letter.' And she mentioned Oswaldo Fernandez in the note you know she addressed it to me, but she mentioned him!

"Well, I took it to where I worked and showed it to everybody, and then I had it hanging on my wall, and then I moved and...well, it went into storage, and I screwed up...It's okay! Someone else has it now, the picture and the letter. I had it, and now someone else has it..."

"I wanted to write a play for Marilyn, not a movie, but a play, once I found out she was into acting. I didn't have any idea for a plot or anything, it was just the idea of her being in a play. And I never get tired of her. I read all the books -- the most fascinating one was, I thought, the one by the woman who'd been her seamstress. It was fascinating: how she'd eat spaghetti in bed, the thing about dying her pubic hair with a toothbrush -- she sounded very real to me, but also very sad. All those little personal things, they don't bother me, in fact they make her real! You know, people tend to 'mythify' stars or writers or baseball players. People refuse to believe they're real. I love the image of DiMaggio sitting there watching television while Marilyn lay there in bed. I'm sad that it was that way, but it's very real. We've all been there...

"The thing was that there was something 'healthy' about someone like Elizabeth Taylor -- that you thought she could take care of herself, healthy in that sense. She could survive, but Marilyn had to be taken care of. I remember an incident with Sophia Loren -- remember when her jewelry got robbed at the hotel here in the city? I had a breakfast appointment for that morning, to talk about this film we were working on, but she'd left a message with my answering service cancelling it the night before. So I called to check with her, and it was right after the robbers had left! She was hysterical of course, but she, too, knew how to take care of herself. She'd been able to describe the robbers to the police and all. Anyhow, after she talked about how they'd acted, how they'd threatened her little boy, she said, 'Now I know why Marilyn Monroe killed herself!' And I said, 'What do you mean?'. And she blurted out, 'It's such a violent country you have no choice!'.

"And the real crime of it with Marilyn I think is that she isn't alive today! She'd still be a superstar -- I'm sure of that. Some of the most beautiful pictures were taken right before she died. I think she'd look great. Sophia says, in her book, that Marilyn was obsessed about aging and she probably was. But she shouldn't have been.

"Could she have been 'saved'? Sophia says she thinks she could've if she'd met her. She says, 'We both rose from the same place...and she is like a sister to me.' And of course I feel like I could've if I tried. But it's a full-time job to save someone like that. Maybe if I'd met her I could have...But if the Strasbergs couldn't...I would've written her things, poems, plays. Sure I could have saved her...just to take her to lunch every once in a while...I've known women like that, who are still around. Not that I saved them...but they just needed some friends, some encouragement. And no one ever called her."

Lenny was right. No one ever called her. And certainly not for herself. That's why she gave up.

Love And All

The interviews for this book were done in the spring and summer of 1980; I handed in the manuscript in September. But I kept an eye on "Marilyn," almost by reflex, clipping pieces that appeared in reference to her, watching the TV listings for movies or whatever. And what a mass of whatever there was? Specials, either about her, or in which she appeared, news items, reminiscences (more!), and even some dirty pictures, although the jury isn't in yet on those.

There was a bit of a flap about that *Penthouse* issue; supposedly Marilyn had made a "blue movie" sometime before 1948, and a Swedish photographer had just "discovered" the film in his files. As far as he and other un-named Swedish "experts" were concerned it was Marilyn fucking and sucking and vibrating away -- of course that was before transistors, so the vibrator was connected to a long wire.

Penthouse ran the pictures, printed in grainy sepia, alongside of standard shots of Marilyn, in an attempt to "match" the faces and bodies. I don't know if it is Marilyn or it isn't. One set of shots seems to match fairly well, in others the likeness isn't that apparent. But why there should be a war of words about the matter is beyond me! Marilyn was scuffling for a living in Hollywood, blue movies were a way to make quick money then as now, and why wouldn't a young would-be star take a job and get paid for doing what she was doing anyway for free, and doing it in the medium she wanted to star in?

On the other hand, it's highly unlikely that the film, once made, would stay hidden this long, if it was really her. Clearly the film-maker would've realized its value and tried to capitalize on it, if not during her lifetime, then after -- and just as the calendar picture had surfaced, so would this have.

But the most interesting thing, again, was that most ordinary people, those who just loved or liked or responded to her, once again said, in effect, "If she did it, okay. Why not?" And some, including me, just thought, "Wow! I'd love to see it!"

It seems to me that dirtier work was done, as usual, by the professionals, the television people, the writers, the entertainment hustlers. I watched a good, honest, intelligent actress named Catherine Hicks play Marilyn in *Marilyn: The Untold Story*, a three-hour long made-for-TV movie shown on ABC. She had the walk, the talk, even, in a lot of shots, the look -- but she wasn't Marilyn! The magic wasn't there, and one had to keep reminding one's self that the real Marilyn was something else again. And the story, based on Mailer's biography, was impossible. As usual it kept giving us the lowdown on her life through scenes that had to be invented, but all was framed in the same old docu-drama fashion in hopes that we'd believe.

They are just never going to learn that originals can't be recreated. Just as Mansfield and Dors and all the rest weren't Marilyn then, Hicks isn't her now. Nor is Frank Converse Joe D., nor Richard Basehart Johnny Hyde, as much as I love both those actors. It all becomes something else—and if you use the impulse to re-create historical figures to make a fiction, i.e., if you build a myth out of the mythic part of the characters, then you've made something people can respond to, and even believe or, God forbid, learn from. If all you're interested in doing is imitating then you'd best remember Joyce Kilmer and his "Only God can make a tree"!

> "I wish I could have done something to stop it from happening, her dying. I know what men mean when they say they could have saved her. That much softness and innocence and sexuality and beauty all together."

I didn't get to see *Fade To Black*, a movie which disappeared pretty quickly, but this also starred a "Marilyn", an Australian actress named Linda Kerridge. The difference here, though, is that Miss Kerridge is used as a look-alike, as a part of the plot, and not as Marilyn herself. The movie may have been a stinker, but that's beside the point. Marilyn did exist as a mythic reality for millions of us, and therefore a writer, screen or otherwise, is certainly justified in trying to use that existence as a focus.

Norman Mailer, on the other hand, has gone the other way. Author of one of the great novels about Hollywood, his *Deer Park*, published some two decades or more ago is a trenchant indictment of exploitation, among other things. But now he's deep into true-life novels or whatever they call them these days, and so he's written a new Marilyn book, in which he invents scenes and puts Marilyn in them. Some are of depravity and violence, but so what. What's more important is that they are all fictions, yet they are presented as reality. Novelists have been building on real models since time began -- I'm sure that Lawrence Sterne knew a Tristam Shandy, a Corparl Trim, an Uncle Toby, and that Richardson knew a Pamela. But they made those people into lasting achetypes, rather than reducing them to less than scale.

Mailer wrote an embarrassing defense of himself for *New York Magazine* which was painful to read. He couched it in the form of a judicial hearing as to his "honesty" in the book, and used the format to insert some of the more purple passages. It was wonderful as an index to where Norman's head is these days, and probably pretty accurate as to the possibilities inherent in as soft an underbelly as Hollywood's, but it ain't Marilyn and why does he need to do that?

I read the piece with more sorrow than anger, simply because Norman Mailer is a better writer than this. He shouldn't have to shrink himself -- or Marilyn. But of course we do live in an age when most people think novels are lies, and non-fiction is truth. Every semester at City College when I begin my creative writing classes there, I have patiently tried to explain that Leo Tolstoy told us more about Russia, and Napoleon's invasion, and love and war than any library full of History and Psychology books, and still no one believes.

So Mailer, riding this wave, produces a Mailer and a Monroe who are less than the reality. Truman Capote I hardly want to mention. Another lost

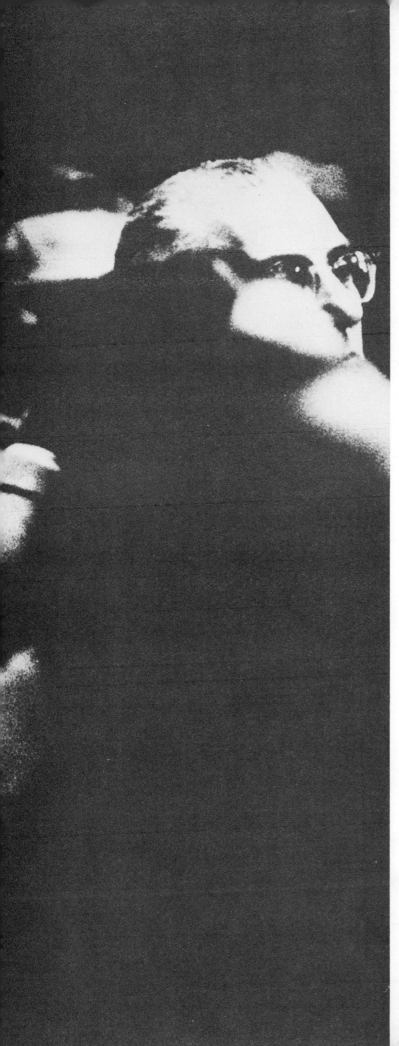

talent, he now merchandises his 'remembrances,' and we buy them. I much prefer my people, remembering how they "met" Marilyn. There's an honesty in those memories that's worth listening to and holding onto.

And just as I was sitting down to write this little postscript to the Marilyn madness, I got a phone call from a young German photographer, who wanted to tell me about a ballet that's scheduled to premiere in Bonn, West Germany, on Valentine's Day. An American choreographer has put together a one and a half hour "biography" for a company of seventeen. Marilyn will be played on alternate nights by two different dancers. One is a ballerina; the other is a man who has made his living imitating Marilyn for the past five years or so in Europe. He is, I was assured, neither a transvestite nor a "camp," though how that can be I don't know. If someone portrays someone of the opposite sex as one's life, I, in my naivete, would assume they were either or both of the above. But that's neither here nor there; what is germane, again, is that I wonder at the value of such a "biography." Why not use that energy to create a "fiction" which might, like "War & Peace," tell us more than reality, since we don't really know what that reality is.

The only ones concerned with the "fiction" -- with what I consider the "real reality," seem to be the poets. Like Lenny and Ed, I'd written a poem for/to Marilyn. Mine was written as near as I can figure in '61. I'd seen, obviously, *The Misfits*, and, equally obviously, Marilyn was still alive. But I never sent mine to her, unfortunately. Not that it would have saved her, but I might have gotten a note like Lenny's. Or, maybe, she would have offered me a date...

As it is, I've had to content myself with my copy of the calendar, some cufflinks in which the calendar pose is preserved in clear plastic, and a Marilyn Monroe bathsheet that some dear friends gave me for Christmas a year or so ago. If you don't think it's hard drying yourself with that wonderful face and body...well, it's a little like the story of the two little ethnics who are walking past Tiffany's when one of them has to relieve himself. His friend says, "So go into Tiffany's! They have to have a men's room, it's the law."

The other little guy goes in, stays five minutes, and rejoins his buddy, and they go off down Fifth Avenue. Two blocks later he has to go again, and his friend says, "You just went in Tiffany's!", and he says, "Well, I'll tell you, I looked at the oaken doors with the gold doorknobs, the marble floors, the onyx urinals, the silver fixtures, and then I looked at me, and, well, I just didn't have the heart..."

So I do manage to dry myself with Marilyn, but it takes every bit of energy I've got. As for the poem, like Lenny I read it to all my friends, and made it a part of my public poetry readings, and kept getting wonderful responses. People kept saying, "Send it to her!" but I was chicken. And so it just stayed part of my work, and I'm sorry now I didn't mail her a copy.

Like Ed's 'testosterone-maddened' verse, this also was a young man's plea. The references are all to *The Misfits* as you're sure to notice -- Gable slipping his hand under the sheet to fondle her as they kissed and the scene faded out was one of my favorite shots in the movie. I didn't work in the one where the camera focusses on her bottom as she and Gable ride horseback, but I sure thought about it a lot.

As for the joke about matzo ball soup, it was a real knee-slapper in the first year or two after she married Arthur. And I really did hate myself every time I told it, but I kept on telling it nevertheless.

I've edited out a section of the poem, given twenty years' hindsight, which had more to do with me and how I lived then than with Marilyn. It just wasn't very good writing, but anybody who's interested can find the complete text in *In Time (Poems 1962-68)* published by Bobbs Merrill.

DEAR MISS MONROE:

everyone else is writing you, why
shouldn/t i? i mean sometimes you
look lovelier than any human on
earth, at such times my heart
goes out to you. believe me
marilyn if i married you i would
never write a movie for you, even
though i/m a writer, and while
interested in sports, i would never
once hit you a home run, i mean
that/s the way i am, the type of
fellow, and the way i feel.

you might like to know, however,
a little more, viz: when i wake
up in the morning, after smoking
a cigarette in bed, and then
peeing, i perform my ablutions,
first, generally, i wash my, no
first i take my vitamin, then i wait
while the water warms up, and then
i wash my hands, and when the water
is warm and my hands too, i wash
my face, and then i dry my hands, but
not my face, unless it/s tuesday and
thursday (on those days i don/t
shave) and then i put on the lavender
shave cream from the shake-em-up bomb.
while that/s setting, i brush my
teeth,with my fingers and colgate,
as my gums won/t stand for a
toothbrush any more, even though
i/ve bought a soft bristle one.
i also clean my glasses at this time,
while the shave cream is sinking
deep. then, after drying my hands
again, and my lips from the tooth
paste, i put on my clean glasses and
begin to shave. up until 1:35 last
saturday i had a chin beard, but now
i only have a mustache. shaving
around the chin area is not a
happy subject these days as it is
very tender. i mentioned this to a
girl the other night, as she happened
to caress me there, on the chin.
after shaving i wet the end of
the towel and use it as a wash

cloth to get the rest of the
foam off me. it smells pretty bad,
i don/t think it/s really lavender,
a house brand from bloch/s drugstore.

that/s how my day begins, on those
days when i get up too late to do
anything but my ablutions before
going to work. i go to work
thirty-five hours a week.

if you promise that your real
image will be the same as your
image on the screen, i probably
will want to marry you. i am a
sports-loving jewish intellectual
writer. some nights i think, while
i/m in bed, of how lovely your
body must be, and i don/t mean of
when the king/s hand is sneaking
under the sheets while you two
kiss, i mean of when you and i
would kiss. thank god i/m not
interested in tits any more, yours
would probably drive me out of
my head. i think i could stay
sane enough with your ass and
belly though to make you reasonably
happy. or else i could write a
poem for you, for your birthday
or our anniversary or whatever.

i remember the story about you
and mrs. miller at pesach, the
one where you said after five
nights, mrs. miller, every night
we have matzo ball soup, is that
the only edible part of the matzo,
the balls? i want you to know
i have told this story, and many
times too, but i never once believed
it, i just told it because it got
a lot of laughs, but inside i hated
myself. i wanted you to know that,
somehow it seemed important
to get that straight.

other things i promise not to do
are: that i won/t shoot rabbits
that are eating our lettuce unless
we need the lettuce to live off,
but i hope that will never come to
pass; 2) i won/t ever buy canned
horsemeat for dog or cat food, although
i am now going (she thinks) with
a girl who has two cats, and though
so far it/s been only tuna fish and
eggs that she serves them, who
knows what she might come up with
next; 3) i will not convert or
attempt to convert you to anything
except more and better me, this
seems fundamental in any marriage.
i want you to know also that i miss
my kids also and could conceive of
such a dumb stunt as gay pulled that
night, sentimentality and all.

this is the first poem i/ve ever
written on my new electric machine,
marilyn, so i must also ask you to
forgive any typographical errors
that creep in, due to my unfamiliarity
with it. the people next door are
getting restless, also, it is late at
night, so that may cut short this
message. in any event, when you
looked at gay in the bar when he
was talking to you, my heart melted.
it/s corny, maybe, to say so, but
gee i sure wish you/d look at me like
that some day. i think something
might come of it. do you like to
drink? i ask only because i like
to drink overly much, like they say,
and would hope that once in a while
you might like to get stoned
with me, instead of me always
going out getting stoned
alone and in secret, or even worse,
having to get stoned with you all the
time. that is, i would hope that you
are the kind would like to get stoned
once in a while with me, and sometimes
would let me get stoned by myself without

getting too bugged about it, but, in
general, that we could plan on going
to bed sober, say, three times a week.

the thought of going to bed with
you reduces me, at this point, to
a jelly, but i am sure that, faced
with you, in the flesh, as it were,
i would forget that you were america/s
beauty queen, and mine, and would find
the wherewithal to produce. i hate
putting it so baldly, but you must
understand by now that this is a problem
you face, i.e., you tend to destroy
any man facing you by psychological
warfare. that/s probably what happened
to arthur, but that/s his problem.

i can only say again that i think i
might learn to love you, and would
certainly cherish the opportunity.
i am at present engaged in polishing
up an essay that is due in two
weeks, and i really must stay with it,
as my tendency is to fuck off whenever
possible, but i certainly would like
to see you if you will be free any time
after the twenty-first, which is when
the essay is due. i will try to write
you a poem in the meantime. yours
very truly, a secret admirer, joel.

Celebrated poet and *Village Voice* columnist since 1969, Joel Oppenheimer was born and raised in Yonkers, New York. He attended Cornell University and the University of Chicago before finding himself at Black Mountain College. He has lived in New York City since 1953, working for fifteen years in print shops before becoming director of the St. Mark's Poetry Project in 1966, one of the liveliest series of readings and workshops on the East Coast, and of New York's Teachers and Writers Collaborative. He is currently poet-in-residence (Distinguished Visiting Professor of Poetry) at the City College of New York.